Absolutely Every*

Bed & Breakfast

*Almost

NEW MEXICO

Absolutely Every*

Bed & Breakfast

*Almost

NEW MEXICO

EDITED BY CARL HANSON

Printed in the United States of America.
Distributed in Canada by Raincoast Books Ltd.
03 02 01 00 99 5 4 3 2 1

Cover design: Jane Jeszeck
Cover illustration: Lisl Dennis/The Image Bank
Interior design and composition: Alan Bernhard
Editor: Carl Hanson
Copy editor: Christine Clifton-Thornton

ISSN 1522-5488
ISBN 1-57061-191-2

Sasquatch Books
615 Second Avenue
Seattle, Washington 98104
(206) 467-4300
books@SasquatchBooks.com
http://www.SasquatchBooks.com

Contents

Absolutely Every Bed & Breakfast Series

Welcome to *Absolutely Every* Bed & Breakfast: New Mexico (*Almost)*, a comprehensive guide to virtually every bed and breakfast establishment in New Mexico. We've done the work for you: Everything you need to know in choosing a bed and breakfast is included on these pages, from architectural style to atmosphere, from price range to breakfast variety. Listings are in alphabetical order by town, so locating the perfect stay at your destination is a snap, and the simple format makes comparing accommodations as easy as turning the page. So whether you're looking for an elegant Victorian inn, a traditional adobe in the heart of pueblo country, or a cozy alpine cottage, *Absolutely Every* Bed & Breakfast: New Mexico (*Almost)* will help you find it.

In addition to New Mexico, the *Absolutely Every* series covers Arizona, Colorado, Northern California, Southern California, Oregon, Washington, and Texas; look for the latest edition of each in your local bookstore. The guides list small- and medium-sized inns, hotels, and host homes that include breakfast in the price of the room. The lists of B&B establishments are compiled from a variety of sources, including directories, chambers of commerce, tourism bureaus, and the World Wide Web. After gathering a complete list, the editors send each innkeeper a survey, asking for basic lodging information and for those special details that set them apart. The completed surveys are then examined and fact-checked for accuracy before inclusion in the book. The **Almost* in the series title reflects the fact that a small number of innkeepers may choose not to be listed, may neglect to respond to the survey and follow-up phone calls, or are not listed because of negative reports received by the editors.

The editors rely on the honesty of the innkeepers in completing the surveys and on feedback from readers to keep the *Absolutely Every Bed & Breakfast* series accurate and up-to-date. (*Note:* While innkeepers are responsible for providing survey information, none are financially connected to the series, nor do they pay any fees to be included in the book.) Please write to us about your experience at any of the bed and breakfasts listed in the series; we'd love to hear from you.

Enjoy your bed and breakfast experience!

—The editors, *Absolutely Every Bed & Breakfast*

How to Use This Book

Absolutely Every Bed & Breakfast: New Mexico is organized alphabetically by town and by establishment name, and includes a comprehensive index. The concise, at-a-glance format of the complete bed and breakfast listings covers fifteen categories of information to help you select just the right bed and breakfast accommodation for your needs. This edition offers you a choice of establishments in cities, towns, and outlying areas.

THE BED & BREAKFAST LISTINGS

Note that although specifics of each establishment have been confirmed by the editors, details such as amenities, decor, and breakfast menus have been provided by the innkeepers. Listings in this guide are subject to change; call to confirm all aspects of your stay, including price, availability, and restrictions, before you go. Some bed and breakfast listings offer only selected information due to lack of response or by request of the innkeeper; complete listings include the following information.

Establishment name
Address: Note that street addresses often vary from actual mailing addresses; confirm the mailing address before sending a reservation payment.
Telephone numbers: Includes any toll-free or fax numbers.
Innkeeper's languages: Languages spoken other than English.
Location: Directions from the nearest town, highway, or landmark.
Open: Notice of any seasonal or other closures.
Description: Overview of architecture, furnishings, landscaping, etc.
Rooms: Number of rooms with private bathrooms vs. shared baths; availability of suites and/or additional guesthouses; and the innkeeper's favorite room.
Rates: Range of room prices, which vary based on private or shared bathroom, season, and individual room amenities. Also noted here are any minimum stay requirements and cancellation policies (usually two weeks' notice is required for a full refund).

Breakfast: Description of breakfast served (full, continental, continental plus, or stocked kitchen).

Credit cards: Indicates which, if any, credit cards are accepted. Note that credit cards may be listed for reservation confirmation purposes only; be prepared to pay by check or cash.

Amenities: Details any special amenities that are included.

Restrictions: Lists any restrictions regarding smoking, children, and pets. Also listed here are any resident pets or livestock.

Awards: Any significant hospitality or historic preservation awards received.

Reviewed: Publications in which the B&B has been reviewed.

Rated: Indicates whether the B&B has been rated by institutions such as the American Automobile Association (AAA), American Bed & Breakfast Association (ABBA), or the Mobil Travel Association.

Member: Indicates membership in any professional hospitality associations or organizations.

Kudos/Comments: Comments from guests who have stayed in the establishment.

ABIQUIU

This is Georgia O'Keeffe country, here in the high desert. Visit O'Keeffe's old haunt at the Ghost Ranch. Investigate the dinosaur pits and the living museum, and Christ in the Desert Monastery. Other areas to explore include Lakes Heron, El Vado, and Abiquiu, the Chama River, Bandelier National Park, and Echo Amphitheatre. Hot local happenings include the Española Onaté Fiesta in the spring, the Apple Festival in September, the Española Rodeo in April and August, the Abiquiu studio tour in October, and Los Posados in December. Native American dances are performed throughout the year. Fifty miles north–northwest of Santa Fe on Highway 84.

CASA DEL RIO

#19946 Highway 84, Chili, NM — *505-753-2035*
Eileen Sopanen, Innkeeper — *FAX 505-753-2035*
Spanish spoken
EMAIL casadelr@roadrunner.com
WEBSITE www.fourcorners.com/nm/inns/casadelrio

LOCATION	Take Highway 84/285 north out of Española for about 10 miles. From milepost 199, go another 0.5 mile.
OPEN	All year
DESCRIPTION	A 1980 pueblo-style adobe compound with Southwest decor including handcarved furniture and local arts and crafts, situated on 12 acres along the Chama River amidst Georgia O'Keeffe's red cliffs.
NO. OF ROOMS	Four rooms with private bathrooms. Try the Casita.
RATES	Year-round rates are $95-125 for a single or double. There is a three-day minimum stay during major holidays, Indian Market, and Northern Pueblos Arts and Crafts Fair. Cancellation requires 21 days' notice.
CREDIT CARDS	MasterCard, Visa
BREAKFAST	Full breakfast is served in the dining room and includes organically grown French roast coffee, tea, juice, Finnish pancakes with apricot compote, eggs Florentine, stuffed French toast with strawberry-raspberry sauce, or cheese blintzes with sour cream and cherry sauce.
AMENITIES	Fresh flowers, wake-up coffee or tea tray, chocolates, horse boarding.
RESTRICTIONS	No smoking, pets are limited to horses, children over 12 are welcome. Hurry Up Shorty is the resident pooch. There are three Arabian horses and sheep.

REVIEWED *Fodor's*

MEMBER New Mexico Bed & Breakfast Association

RATED AAA 3 Diamonds

Old Abiquiu Bed & Breakfast

Abiquiu, NM 87510 *505-685-4784*

Alamogordo

Cottonwood Inn Bed & Breakfast

1204 New York Avenue, Alamogordo, NM 88310 *505-437-6761*

Albuquerque

This mile-high city in the shadow of the Sandia Mountains is the home of the University of New Mexico, the New Mexico State Fair in September, and the world's largest balloonist gathering, called the Balloon Fiesta, in early October (make those reservations well in advance for the great balloon gala, as rooms fill up in a hurry). Don't miss Old Town, Sandia Peak Tramway, Rio Grande Nature Center, Petroglyph National Monument, Maxwell Museum of Anthropology, Indian Pueblo Cultural Center, and the tours of Christmas luminarias. The Turquoise Trail drive, through area ghost towns, is nice and scenic, and the Albuquerque Aquarium and Botanical Gardens are worth visiting as well. Local events feature the Gathering of Nations Pow Wow in April and juried arts and crafts fairs in June and November.

Adobe & Roses Bed & Breakfast

1011 Ortega Road NW, Albuquerque, NM 87114 *505-898-0654*
Dorothy Morse, Resident Owner
Spanish spoken
WEBSITE www.virtualcities.com

LOCATION	From the north, take the Tramway/4th Street exit. Continue on 4th Street about 4 miles to Ortega Road. Turn right, go 0.7 mile to the private gravel drive across from the blue mailbox, and turn right. From the south, east, or west, get off at the Rio Grande Boulevard exit, go north 6 miles on Rio Grande to Ortega Road, and turn right.
OPEN	All year
DESCRIPTION	A spacious 1950s Santa Fe adobe and a separate adobe guesthouse with tilework and fireplaces, on 2 semirural acres with extensive gardens.
NO. OF ROOMS	Three rooms with private bathrooms. Pick the big suite.
RATES	Year-round rates are $55-89 for a single or double with a private bathroom, $79-89 for a suite, and $130 for the two bedroom guesthouse. There is a two-night minimum stay, four nights during Balloon Fiesta, and cancellation requires two weeks' notice.
CREDIT CARDS	No
BREAKFAST	Full breakfast is served in the dining room, guestrooms, or guesthouse portal and includes French roast coffee and either muffins and fruit, eggs and potatoes, pancakes, or waffles. "I can accommodate people's time and what type of breakfast they like (hearty or light)."
AMENITIES	Flowers, terry robes, fireplaces, kitchenettes, use of washer/dryer, early morning coffee delivered, bird feeders, extensive library, lily pond, occasional classical music affairs, off-street parking, piano in big suite, phones, TV/VCR, hair dryers, individual heating and cooling.
RESTRICTIONS	No smoking. There is a Shelty named Laddie, two cats named Rosie and Emma Dingbat, two boarded horses, fish in the fish-pond, a resident roadrunner, and a number of hens and golden pheasants.
REVIEWED	*Recommended Country Inns—The Southwest; Best Places to Stay in the Southwest; The Southwest's Best Bed & Breakfasts; America's Best Bed & Breakfasts*
KUDOS/COMMENTS	"Two lovely guesthouses in spectacular gardens (Dorothy makes me think I should give up gardening, they're so gorgeous). Warm and congenial hostess." "Elegant yet homey, charming, old adobe home with two casitas. Warm hospitality, delicious food and just a marvelous feeling of an "enchanted getaway." (1996)

Adobe Garden at Los Ranchos

641 Chavez NW, Albuquerque, NM 87107 *505-345-1954*
Lee & Tricia Smith, Resident Owners
Japanese spoken

LOCATION	From I-40, take Rio Grande north 3.9 miles, turn right (east) on Chavez, and go 0.7 mile. The B&B is on the northeast corner of Chavez and Guadalupe Trail.
OPEN	All year
DESCRIPTION	A two-story 1939 pueblo-style revivalist adobe on 3 acres with gardens and mountain views. Furnished with internationally acquired antiques.
NO. OF ROOMS	Three rooms with private bathrooms and three rooms in the bunkhouse share one bathroom. Pick the Kiva Room.
RATES	Winter rate for a single or double is $89; summer rates are $95-115. The bunkhouse is $150 year-round. There is no minimum stay and cancellation requires two weeks' notice.
CREDIT CARDS	No
BREAKFAST	Continental plus is served in the dining room or guesthouse and includes a variety of baked breads with fresh fruit from the orchard and sometimes eggs from the owner's black hens.
AMENITIES	Afternoon tea, outdoor swimming pool, flower and herb gardens, air conditioning, fireplaces in most guestrooms, wood stoves and fireplaces in public rooms, use of family library.
RESTRICTIONS	No smoking, no pets, children over 10 are welcome. The resident pets are chickens and turkeys.

Anderson's Victorian B&B

11600 Modesto Avenue NE, Albuquerque, NM 87122 *505-856-6211*
WEBSITE www.bbhost.com/andersonsvictorian/

BOTTGER MANSION

110 San Felipe NW, Albuquerque, NM 87104 — *505-243-3639*
Yvonne & Ron Koch, Innkeepers — *800-758-3639*
Spanish spoken — *FAX 505-243-4378*
EMAIL BottgerK@aol.com — *WEBSITE www.Bottger.com*

LOCATION	In historic Old Town near the south entrance on the corner of San Felipe and Central Boulevard (old Route 66).
OPEN	All year
DESCRIPTION	A 1912 three-story American four square with Victorian furnishings, hardwood and marble floors; listed on the National Historic Register.
NO. OF ROOMS	Eight rooms with private bathrooms.
RATES	Year-round rates for a single or double are $99-179. There is no minimum stay and cancellation requires 20 days' notice and a $40 fee.
CREDIT CARDS	American Express, Diners Club, Discover, MasterCard, Visa
BREAKFAST	Full gourmet breakfast is served in the dining room and includes coffee, teas, juices, yogurt, hot entrees such as Swedish pancakes and "crunchy French toast."
AMENITIES	A soda fountain is available at all times and includes crushed ice, coffee and tea, evening wine and hors d'oeuvres, shaded grass and marble courtyards with patio tables and chairs, individually controlled heating and cooling, Jacuzzi.
RESTRICTIONS	No smoking, no pets
REVIEWED	*The Official Guide to American Historic Inns*
MEMBER	Albuquerque Bed & Breakfast Association
RATED	AAA 2 Diamonds

BRITTANIA & W. E. MAUGER ESTATE

701 Roma Avenue NW, Albuquerque, NM 87102 — *505-242-8755*
Mark & Keith, Innkeepers — *800-719-9189*
EMAIL maugerbb@awl.com — *FAX 505-842-8835*

LOCATION	From I-25, take the Martin Luther King exit. At the light, head west for 2 miles through downtown to 7th. Turn right and go 1 block.

OPEN	All year
DESCRIPTION	An 1897 three-story Queen Anne Victorian with eclectic Victorian decor, listed on the National and State Historic Registers.
NO. OF ROOMS	Eight rooms with private bathrooms.
RATES	Year-round rates are $89-179 for a single or double. There is a minimum stay during the Balloon Fiesta and cancellation requires 10 days' notice.
CREDIT CARDS	American Express, Diners Club, Discover, MasterCard, Visa
BREAKFAST	Full Southwest-style breakfast is served in the dining room. The specialty is green chile eggs Benedict.
AMENITIES	Flowers, robes, phones, evening wine and cheese, snack basket in rooms, complimentary beverages, air conditioning, small refrigerator in each room, down comforters, 4 blocks to the business district and Old Town.
RESTRICTIONS	No smoking. Nellie and Barney are the resident pooches.
REVIEWED	*Frommer's; Fodor's*
MEMBER	New Mexico Bed & Breakfast Association, Professional Association of Innkeepers International, Inn Points Worldwide

CANYON CREST

5804 Canyon Crest, Albuquerque, NM 87111 *505-821-4898*

CASA DEL GRANJERO

414 C de Baca Lane NW, Albuquerque, NM 87114 *505-897-4144*
Victoria & Butch Farmer, Resident Owners *800-701-4144*
Spanish and Italian spoken *FAX 505-897-9788*
EMAIL *granjero@cwix.com* WEBSITE *www.innewmexico.com*

LOCATION	From the airport, take I-25 north to the Alameda exit (233). Go west on Alameda to 4th Street, turn left onto 4th Street for 0.2 mile. Turn right on to C de Baca Lane and drive to the last house on the left.
OPEN	All year
DESCRIPTION	An 1880 territorial adobe hacienda and guesthouse with very large rooms, Mexican tile, vegas and corbels, and skylights, situated on 3 acres with walled courtyards and gardens.

NO. OF ROOMS	Seven rooms with private bathrooms.
RATES	Year-round rates for a single or double are $79-119, $109-159 for a suite, and $79-159 for the guesthouse. There is a two-night minimum stay during weekends, three nights during holidays and events, and cancellation requires 14 days' notice for a full refund.
CREDIT CARDS	American Express, Discover, MasterCard, Visa
BREAKFAST	Full breakfast is served in the dining room or in the guestrooms by request and includes juice or nectars, coffee, tea, milk, hearty entrée, custard, blueberry coffeecake, fresh fruit, and always seconds. Lunch, dinner, and special meals are available by arrangement only.
AMENITIES	Flowers, robes, bath amenities, hot tub, sauna, massage, candy, cookies, snacks, open kitchen, beverages, horse boarding, music, fireplaces, large-screen TV, hiking trails, cooking classes, romance packages, meeting facilities, fully equipped office with Internet access.
RESTRICTIONS	Smoking outdoors only. The barn cats are called Raven and Fluffy; the pigmy goats are Ambrose, Joycie, and Nancy; and the quarter horses are Chinda and Sweetheart.
REVIEWED	*Fodor's; Frommer's; America's Wonderful Little Hotels & Inns*
MEMBER	New Mexico Bed & Breakfast Association, American Bed & Breakfast Association, Professional Association of Innkeepers International
RATED	AAA 3 Diamonds, Mobil 3 Stars
KUDOS/COMMENTS	"Beautifully decorated southwest establishment with excellent breakfasts." "Beautiful, spacious." (1996) "A real B&B run by real people: open, warm, friendly, and knowledgeable." (1999)

Casas de Suenos Old Town Bed & Breakfast Inn

310 Rio Grande Boulevard SW, Albuquerque, NM 87104 *505-247-4560*
Spanish spoken *505-842-8493*
WEBSITE www.travelbase.com/destinations/albuquerque/casas

LOCATION	From the intersection of I-25 and I-40, take I-40 1.5 miles to the Rio Grande Boulevard exit. Turn left, going south on Rio Grande. Continue on Rio Grande past Old Town and Central Avenue. Go an additional 1.5 blocks to the end of Rio Grande; the B&B is on the left-hand side.
OPEN	All year

DESCRIPTION	A 1940 historic country inn on 2 acres of country gardens. Listed on the National Historic Register and decorated with antiques and original art.
NO. OF ROOMS	Twenty-one rooms and adobe suites with private bathrooms.
RATES	Please inquire about current rates and cancellation information.
CREDIT CARDS	American Express, Carte Blanche, Diners Club, Discover, MasterCard, Visa
BREAKFAST	Full breakfast is served in the dining room or guestrooms and changes daily. Breakfast includes fruits, cereals, hot and cold drinks, pastries, jams, and a hot entrée cooked to order, usually two choices. Lunch, dinner, and vegetarian room service is available.
AMENITIES	Individual temperature control, modems, concierge service, robes, hot tubs, resident massage therapists, cable TV/VCR, fireplaces, kitchens, gardens with waterfalls.
RESTRICTIONS	No smoking, no pets, children over 14 are welcome.
REVIEWED	*Access Santa Fe, Taos & Albuquerque; America's Wonderful Little Hotels & Inns*
MEMBER	Professional Association of Innkeepers International, American Bed & Breakfast Association
RATED	ABBA 2 Crowns, Mobil 3 Stars
AWARDS	1991, One of America's Great Country Inns, Discovery Channel
KUDOS/COMMENTS	"Wonderful breakfasts. Beautiful gardens & private casitas, friendly staff." (1996)

Casita Chamisa Bed & Breakfast

850 Chamisal Road NW, Albuquerque, NM 87107 *505-897-4644*
WEBSITE www.southwesterninns.com/chamisa.htm

KUDOS/COMMENTS	"Wonderful two-bedroom guesthouse, archeological site, great hosts & breakfasts." "It's our favorite place to stay in Albuquerque." (1996)

Cinnamon Morning

2700 Rio Grande Boulevard NW, Albuquerque, NM 87104 *505-345-3541*
Sue & Dick Percihick, Innkeepers *800-214-9481*
Some Spanish spoken *FAX 505-342-2283*
EMAIL dpercihick@aol.com *WEBSITE www.cinnamonmorning.com*

LOCATION Exit I-40 at Rio Grande and turn right at the bottom of the ramp. Go exactly 1 mile. The B&B is the fourth house after the Matthew traffic light.

OPEN All year

DESCRIPTION A 1950s-era contemporary New Mexican host home that combines colorful decorating with contemporary furnishings and antiques.

NO. OF ROOMS Four rooms with private bathrooms and two rooms share one bathroom.

RATES Year-round rates are $70-105 for a single or double with a private bathroom. The two-bedroom guesthouse is $160. There is a three-day minimum stay during the Balloon Fiesta and holidays, and cancellation requires one week's notice.

CREDIT CARDS American Express, Discover, MasterCard, Visa

BREAKFAST Full breakfast is served in the dining room or outdoors on the covered patio and includes juice, coffee, hot teas, fresh fruit, breads and muffins, and entrées that include regional specialties. Dietary restrictions may be accommodated with advance notice. Resident chickens provide fresh eggs.

AMENITIES Air conditioning, on-site parking, outdoor fireplace, outdoor hot tub, robes, hair dryers, extensive library, movies, CDs, outdoor kitchen, six months of the year all meals are cooked and served outdoors next to the stuffed zebra, meetings and retreats hosted with full food service (no alcohol).

RESTRICTIONS No smoking inside, pets considered (please call), children are welcome in the guesthouse. Santo is the Lhasa apso; Noodle, Missffit, and Purrffect are the cats. There are chickens and a peacock that courts the chickens.

REVIEWED *Frommer's Santa Fe, Taos, & Albuquerque*

MEMBER Albuquerque Bed & Breakfast Association, New Mexico Bed & Breakfast Association

KUDOS/COMMENTS "Truly a home visit. Sparkling clean, interesting decor, comfortable surroundings, gardens, outdoor kitchen like Old Mexico, most of all generous and fun loving hosts. They embody mi casa su casa."

The Corner House

9121 James Place NE, Albuquerque, NM 87111 *505-298-5800*
Jean F. Thompson, Resident Owner

LOCATION	From I-25 going south, exit on Paseo del Norte and go east to Wyoming past Montgomery. The second left is James
OPEN	All year
DESCRIPTION	A 1972 Southwest-style host home with an eclectic decor that includes some antiques, located in a quiet residential neighborhood with a view of the Sandia Mountains.
NO. OF ROOMS	Two rooms with private bathrooms and two rooms share one bathroom. Try the Wedgewood Room.
RATES	Year-round rates for a single or double with a private bathroom are \$45-60 and a single or a double with a shared bathroom is \$35-45. There is no minimum stay and cancellation requires 14 days' notice.
CREDIT CARDS	No
BREAKFAST	Full breakfast is served in the dining room and includes grapefruit or juice, an egg dish, fresh fruit garnish, muffin, coffee, and tea. Dinner is also available.
AMENITIES	Flowers in season, fresh herbs, pillow candy, soaps, shampoo, extra towels, evaporative cooling, two rooms have small refrigerators and telephones.
RESTRICTIONS	No smoking. Children are welcome. The resident dogs are Smiley, "sort of a Lab," and Cory, "sort of a blue heeler."
REVIEWED	*Bed & Breakfast U.S.A.*

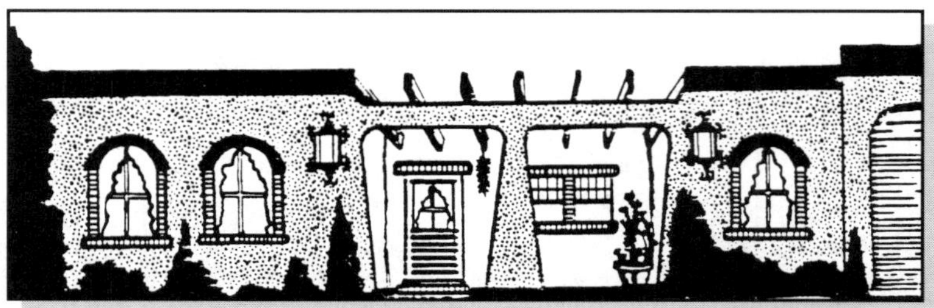

The Corner House, Albuquerque

Devonshire Adobe Inn

4801 All Saints Road NW, Albuquerque, NM 87120 — *505-898-3366*
Jay & Pat Power, Resident Owners — *800-240-1149*
EMAIL devon@nmia.com — *FAX 505-898-8793*
WEBSITE www.devonshireadobeinn.com

LOCATION	From I-25, head west on Paseo del Norte to Eagle Ranch Road. Turn left (south), go 1 block, turn left again, and drive 0.3 mile.
OPEN	All year
DESCRIPTION	A 1996 two-story northern New Mexico inn with Victorian decor, an atrium with a skylight, and a dining room that opens onto a garden.
NO. OF ROOMS	Seven rooms with private bathrooms. Try the Alexander.
RATES	During the first two weeks in October, rates are $110-150 for a single or double. The remainder of the year, rates are $80-130 for a single or double. There is a three-day minimum stay from October 1 through October 15, and cancellation requires 14 days' notice, 45 days from October 1 through October 15.
CREDIT CARDS	American Express, Diners Club, Discover, MasterCard, Visa
BREAKFAST	Full breakfast is served in the dining room and includes egg specialties such as coddled eggs and omelets, crepes, coffee, tea, and cereals.
AMENITIES	Two sittings for afternoon tea Tuesday through Friday; four common rooms; antiques; spectacular views of the mountains, city, and bosque; TVs and refrigerators available upon request, phones in each room; handicapped accessible room; parking; air conditioning.
RESTRICTIONS	No smoking, no pets
MEMBER	New Mexico Bed & Breakfast Association, Albuquerque Bed & Breakfast Association
RATED	AAA 3 Diamonds
AWARDS	1997, four star rating for the tea room, *Albuquerque Journal*
KUDOS/COMMENTS	"Excellent food, well run."

Enchanted Vista Bed & Breakfast

10700 Del Rey Avenue NE, Albuquerque, NM 87122 — *505-823-1301*
Tillie Gonzales, Resident Owner

Hacienda Antigua Bed & Breakfast

6708 Tierra Drive NW, Albuquerque, NM 87107 — *505-345-5399*
Ann Dunlap and Melinda Moffitt, Resident Owners — *800-484-2385, code 9954*
EMAIL antigua@swcp.com
WEBSITE www.haciendantigua.com

LOCATION	From the intersection of I-25 and I-40, take I-25 north 4.2 miles to exit 231. Go left on Osuna Road, drive 2.4 miles, cross the railroad tracks, and turn right on Tierra. Watch for B&B sign on right.
OPEN	All year
DESCRIPTION	A 1790 hacienda with 19th century antiques.
NO. OF ROOMS	Five rooms with private bathrooms.
RATES	Year-round rates for a single or double are $85-95 and the suite is $125-135. Holidays and Balloon Fiesta rates are higher. There is a two-night minimum stay on weekends during high season and three nights during Balloon Fiesta. Ask about the cancellation policy
CREDIT CARDS	American Express, Discover, MasterCard, Visa
BREAKFAST	Full breakfast is served in the dining room, guestrooms, or on the patio and includes an entrée that changes daily, accompanied by fresh fruit, hot breads, granola, and sausage or bacon, juice, and coffee.
AMENITIES	Afternoon refreshments, refrigerators, fireplaces in rooms, antique clawfoot tubs, outdoor hot tub, swimming pool, garden, and orchard sitting area.
RESTRICTIONS	No smoking, no pets, children over six are welcome.
REVIEWED	*Frommer's Santa Fe, Taos, & Albuquerque; Country Inns* magazine
MEMBER	New Mexico Bed & Breakfast Association, Professional Association of Innkeepers International
RATED	Mobil 3 Stars
KUDOS/COMMENTS	"Wonderful architecture, great hospitality. A step into the past to experience New Mexico." "Classic adobe hacienda with excellent restoration by owners. Part was originally a chapel. Quiet, safe and easy to get to." "Beautifully restored, Old World flavor, gracious hosts." "This adobe is one of the best examples of the traditional architecture, well maintained and appointed." (1996) "Old hacienda, beautifully appointed with lots of character and charm. Wonderful hosts." "Historical hacienda, romantic getaway, very comfortable, great innkeepers." (1999)

Hacienda de Colores

1113 Montoya NW, Albuquerque, NM 87104 — *505-247-0013*
Suzana Francis, Innkeeper — *877-265-6737*
Spanish spoken — *FAX 505-242-7063*
EMAIL Hdecolores@aol.com

LOCATION	Five minutes from the Old Town Plaza and 10 minutes from the center of downtown.
OPEN	All year
DESCRIPTION	A 1998 old adobe–style Spanish hacienda with old Spanish–style decor, nestled on a 6 pastoral acres amongst ageless native trees.
NO. OF ROOMS	Two rooms with private bathrooms. Try the Country Room.
RATES	Year-round rates are $100-185 for a single or double. There is no minimum stay and cancellation requires two weeks' notice.
CREDIT CARDS	American Express, MasterCard, Visa
BREAKFAST	Full breakfast is cooked to order.
AMENITIES	Meeting facilities, air conditioning, handicapped accessible, wine and hors d'oeuvres, Jacuzzi in each room.
RESTRICTIONS	No smoking, no pets. There are horses on the property.

The Inn at Paradise

10035 Country Club Lane NW, Albuquerque, NM 87114 — *505-898-6161*
Charles "Lefty" Brinkman, Innkeeper — *800-938-6161*
Some French and German spoken — *FAX 505-890-1090*
WEBSITE www.innatparadise.com

LOCATION	From the airport, head north on I-25 and take the Paseo del Norte exit. Head west until the road dead-ends at Golf Course Road. Turn right and drive 1.3 miles. Turn left onto Country Club Lane and enter the golf course. The inn is the first building on the left.
OPEN	All year
DESCRIPTION	A renovated 1994 two-story Spanish inn featuring original artwork on consignment from local artists.
NO. OF ROOMS	Sixteen rooms with private bathrooms.
RATES	Year-round rates are $50-80 for a single or double. There is no minimum stay.
CREDIT CARDS	American Express, Discover, MasterCard, Visa

BREAKFAST	Continental plus is served in the dining room and includes juices, fresh fruit in season, hot and cold cereal, excellent toast, jam, peanut butter, coffee, tea, milk, hot chocolate, and hot cider. Lunch, dinner, and catered meals are also available.
AMENITIES	Hot tub in garden, golf packages, meeting room (as well as a bar and restaurant) next door at the golf club.
RESTRICTIONS	No smoking. Pets are welcome. KoKo is the resident "pure-bred pound dog. He's been to hotel school and golfs every day."
REVIEWED	*Pets Welcome; Fodor's*

Jazz Inn Bed & Breakfast

111 Walter NE, Albuquerque, NM 87102
Sophia & Nicholas Peron, Resident Owners
Polish spoken
505-242-1530
888-JAZZ-INN
FAX 505-242-1530
WEBSITE www.jazzinn.com

LOCATION	From I-25, take Central Avenue 0.4 mile west to Walter; go north on Walter to the inn.
OPEN	All year
DESCRIPTION	A 1900-era southwestern Victorian inn with eclectic furnishings.
NO. OF ROOMS	Five rooms with private bathrooms and two rooms have half-baths and share bathing facilities. Pick the Duke Ellington Suite.
RATES	Please inquire about current rates. There is a three-night minimum stay during the October Ballon Fiesta. Ask about the cancellation policy.
CREDIT CARDS	American Express, Carte Blanche, Diners Club, Discover, JCB, MasterCard, Visa
BREAKFAST	Continental plus is served in the guestrooms or the kitchen and includes huevos rancheros with pinto beans, green chili, Taos eggs and potatoes, cereal, fruit, and juice. Special meals are available on request.
AMENITIES	Grand piano, library, 5,000 LP library, contemporary New Mexico arts and crafts, sculpture garden, jazz memorabilia, occasional live jazz, handicapped accessible.
RESTRICTIONS	Smoking outside only. The resident "pound" dog is called P. D. Girl.
AWARDS	Best Neighborhood Revitalization Project, Albuquerque Conservation Association

Jenna's B&B

3020 Carlota Road NW, Albuquerque, NM 87104 *505-242-3833*

La Perla Bed & Breakfast Casita

409½ 19th Street NW, Albuquerque, NM 87104 *505-246-1637*
Phyllis & Rob Rispoli, Innkeepers *888-807-3752*
Some Spanish spoken *FAX 505-246-1616*
EMAIL phrassoc@aol.com *WEBSITE www.laperlabedandbreakfast.com*

LOCATION	From the airport, take I-25 north 2.7 miles to the Lomas exit. Turn left onto Lomas, drive 1.8 miles to 17th Street, turn right, and drive 1 block to Marble. Turn left, drive 2 blocks until Marble dead-ends at 19th. Turn right and drive until you see La Perla's tile sign on the left. From I-40, exit at Rio Grande Boulevard. Turn south onto Rio Grande and drive approximately 0.5 mile to Mountain. Turn left, drive to 19th Street (second stoplight), turn right, drive 1 long block, then make a quick jog to the right across Old Town Road, staying on 19th. La Perla is the second house on your right.
OPEN	All year
DESCRIPTION	A restored 1900 southwest adobe casita done in warm, soft blues and reds "that make everyone feel at home." This private casita is set in the heart of Albuquerque's Old Town Historic District.
NO. OF ROOMS	One room with a private bathroom and two rooms share one bathroom.
RATES	April through October, rates are \$89-149 for a single or double. November through March, rates are \$79-119 for a single or double. Cancellation requires one week's notice.
CREDIT CARDS	American Express, MasterCard, Visa
BREAKFAST	Full healthy, hearty breakfast is served in the guestrooms or courtyard and is made with organic and whole-grain ingredients. Special requests are happily accommodated, with notice.
AMENITIES	Private casita; concierge services; airport pick-up may be available; kitchen stocked with snacks, cold drinks, and wine; guests can cook own evening meals; washer/dryer; private telephone line.
RESTRICTIONS	No smoking. Bear is the resident Lab. Bear is "all bark, no bite" and is not allowed in the casita.
MEMBER	Albuquerque Bed & Breakfast Association

La Posada de Albuquerque

125 2nd Street NW, Albuquerque, NM 87102 — *505-242-9090*
FAX 505-242-8664

Los Ranchos Bed & Breakfast

641 Chavez Road Northwest, Albuquerque, NM 87107 — *505-345-7058*

Maggie's Raspberry Ranch, A Bed & Breakfast

9817 Eldridge Road NW, Albuquerque, NM 87114 — *505-897-1523*
Margaret Lilley, Resident Owner — *800-897-1523*
FAX 505-897-1523

LOCATION	From I-25 north, take exit 233 left on Alameda and go 3.2 miles to Rio Grande North. Take the second left (Western Meadows) and then the first right, on Eldridge. The B&B is the third house on the left.
OPEN	All year
DESCRIPTION	A 1965 two-story ranch-style host home with contemporary country furnishings.
NO. OF ROOMS	Two rooms with private bathrooms and three rooms share two bathrooms.
RATES	Year-round rates for a double with a private or shared bathroom are $75-95. There is a two-night minimum stay during weekends and cancellation requires 10 days' notice, 30 days during the Balloon Fiesta.
CREDIT CARDS	MasterCard, Visa
BREAKFAST	Full breakfast is served in the dining room and always includes raspberries and other fruit, home-baked breads, hot cereals, baked egg dishes, pancakes, waffles, coffee, tea, juices, and "special surprises—cook's choice."
AMENITIES	Covered heated pool, hot tub, Jacuzzi, robes, mapped routes of day trips from Albuquerque.

RESTRICTIONS No smoking. "We do allow children of all ages and pets (parents are welcome too)."

MEMBER Albuquerque Bed & Breakfast Association

OLD TOWN BED & BREAKFAST

---

707 17th Street NW, Albuquerque, NM 87104 *505-764-9144*
Nancy Hoffman, Resident Owner *888-900-9144*
WEBSITE *www.virtualcities.com*

LOCATION From I-25, go west on Lomas Boulevard to 17th Street, then go north to 707, midway on the left. From I-40, go south on Rio Grande Boulevard, east on Mountain, to 19th Street. Turn right onto Old Town Road and take a left, then an immediate right onto 17th Street.

OPEN All year

DESCRIPTION A 1940 Pueblo-style adobe home featuring traditional ceilings of genuine vigas and latillas and an interior furnished with American and European antiques with southwestern touches, situated in a quiet, tree-shaded neighborhood.

NO. OF ROOMS One room with a private bathroom and one room shares a bathroom.

RATES Year-round rate for a single or double with a private bathroom is $70, the suite with the shared bathroom is $85. There is no minimum stay and cancellation requires 10 days' notice.

CREDIT CARDS No

BREAKFAST Full breakfast is served in the dining room or on the patio and includes fresh-squeezed orange juice, a fruit entrée, home-baked goods including muffins, cobblers, or coffeecake, omelets or other egg dishes, and fresh-ground coffee.

AMENITIES Refreshments (beverages and homemade cookies) in room upon arrival, robes, Jacuzzi tub and kiva fireplace in suite, ceiling fans, special remembrances (birthdays, anniversaries) with advance notice, early morning coffee, early breakfast for early departures, daily newspaper, fresh flowers.

RESTRICTIONS No smoking, no pets. All children will be considered (prefer children five and over).

REVIEWED *Journey to the High Southwest; Complete Guide to Bed & Breakfasts; Fodor's; Hidden Southwest; Lonely Planet*

MEMBER Albuquerque Bed & Breakfast Association

KUDOS/COMMENTS "Lovely, cultured innkeepers with good taste. Moderate rates. Walking distance from Old Town." "Near historic district, caring hostess in a quiet, secluded area." "Innkeeper Nancy Hoffman is a sharp lady and great cook. Her two room inn has great flavor of the Southwest." "Small, friendly, typical old New Mexico adobe, shade trees, comfortable." (1996) "Quaint, tasteful B&B with a gracious hostess."

Potteries Bed & Breakfast

4100 Dietz Farm Circle NW, Albuquerque, NM 87107 *505-344-3144*

The Ranchette Bed & Breakfast

2329 Lakeview Road SW, Albuquerque, NM 87105 *505-877-5140*
Janis Hildebrand, Resident Owner

Rio Grande House

3100 Rio Grande Boulevard NW, Albuquerque, NM 87107 *505-345-0120*
WEBSITE www.bbhost.com:8008/riogrande

Sarabande Bed & Breakfast

5637 Rio Grande Boulevard NW, Albuquerque, NM 87107 *505-345-4923*

KUDOS/COMMENTS "Very nice furnishings, good taste, nice gardens, very nice ladies run it. A bit formal for certain people." "Lovely, easy to find and many amenities." "Lovely territorial B&B, outdoor lap pool and spa. Wonderful food and gracious hosts." "Beautiful contemporary Southwest-style B&B in the north valley." "Bright and sunny, beautifully appointed B&B." "Superior services."

Silver Hill Bed & Breakfast

1815 Silver SE, Albuquerque, NM 87106 *505-764-8464*
Cathy W., Innkeeper
EMAIL silverhillbnb@iolnm.net
WEBSITE www.iolnm.net/silverhillbnb

LOCATION From the airport, go south on Yale to Gibson. At Gibson (the first light), take a left and go to University (the next light), turn north on University. Staying on University, go past three lights before turning right onto Silver.

OPEN All year

DESCRIPTION A 1923 bungalow decorated in a comfortable style with quilts (no lace or satin). Listed on the National and State Historic Registers.

NO. OF ROOMS Two rooms share one bathroom.

RATES Year-round rates are $55-70 for a single or double. There is a two-night minimum stay. Ask about a cancellation policy.

CREDIT CARDS American Express, Discover, MasterCard, Visa

BREAKFAST Guests choose either full or continental breakfast. The hostess inquires about special dietary needs at check-in.

AMENITIES Shampoo and shower soap; robes; pedestrian neighborhood wonderful for walks in the morning or evening; central heat and air conditioning; flower garden in the front with spring, summer, and fall flowers.

RESTRICTIONS No smoking, children over five are welcome. Honey is the resident cat. "She likes to sit out and be social with the guests and especially likes to have her head scratched. I try not to let her into guest rooms or the bathroom."

REVIEWED *Stash Tea*

A Unitarian Bed & Breakfast

3015 Quincy NE, Albuquerque, NM 87110 *505-883-0368*
Cora Cooper, Resident Owner
Some Spanish spoken

LOCATION Three blocks from intersection of San Mateo and Candelaria, 4 blocks north of I-40.

OPEN All year

DESCRIPTION A 1952 adobe host home with southwestern furnishings.

NO. OF ROOMS Two rooms with private bathrooms and one room shares a bathroom.

RATES Year-round rates for a single or double with a private or shared bathroom are $15-30. There is no minimum stay and no cancellation policy.

CREDIT CARDS No

BREAKFAST A healthy breakfast is served in the dining room or on the patio.

AMENITIES Tour advice and literature on the Southwest.

RESTRICTIONS No smoking, no pets, children over 12 are welcome. The resident cats were rescued from abandonment.

VISTA DE ALBUQUERQUE

5336 Canada Vista Place NW, Albuquerque, NM 87120 *505-899-9301*

W. J. MARSH HOUSE VICTORIAN B&B

301 Edith SE, Albuquerque, NM 87102 *505-247-1001*
Janice Lee Sperling, Resident Owner *888-956-2774*
French and Spanish spoken *FAX 505-842-5109*
WEBSITE www.marshhouse.com

LOCATION From I-25, take the Martin Luther King exit, turn west and drive 4 short blocks to Edith. Turn left and go 4 blocks to the corner of Silver and Edith.

OPEN All year

DESCRIPTION A restored 1892 three-story Queen Anne Victorian with Victorian furnishings. The B&B is on both the State and National Historic Registers.

NO. OF ROOMS Two rooms with private bathrooms and four rooms with shared bathrooms.

RATES Please inquire about current rates and cancellation information.

CREDIT CARDS MasterCard, Visa

BREAKFAST Full gourmet breakfast is served in the dining room. Lunch, teas, and picnics are also available. Special requests, such as diabetic or vegetarian diets, can be accommodated with one week's notice.

AMENITIES	Fresh mints, an old-fashioned alarm clock, reading materials appropriate to the Southwest, writing paper and pens, hypoallergenic pillows, robes in rooms with shared baths.
RESTRICTIONS	No smoking, no pets, children over 10 are welcome. "Sorry, we are not wheelchair accessible." Pepper is the resident pooch, and there are three cats.
REVIEWED	*Fodor's; Inn Places*
MEMBER	New Mexico Bed & Breakfast Association, Albuquerque Bed & Breakfast Association, Professional Association of Innkeepers International
KUDOS/COMMENTS	"Nice accommodations, congenial hosts." (1996)

ALTO

CASA DEL COCINERO

Highway 48, Alto, NM 88312 — *505-336-7815*

ANGEL FIRE

Surrounded by Carson National Forest, in the Sangre de Cristo Mountains, Angel Fire is a year-round resort town, best known for its alpine skiing. Enjoy the Balloon Festival in July and Paul Bunyan Days in September, and don't miss the thrills and spills of the World Champion Shovel Races. Nearby Eagle Nest Lake boasts excellent trout fishing.

HILL HOUSE BED & BREAKFAST

10 Via del Rey, Angel Fire, NM 87710 — *505-377-6055*
800-621-2965

MONTE VERDE RANCH B&B

PO Box 173, Angel Fire, NM 87710 — *505-377-6928*
Laura Lou Fuller & Sally LeBus, Resident Owners

Wildflower Bed & Breakfast, Angel Fire

WILDFLOWER BED & BREAKFAST

40 Halo Pines Terrace, Angel Fire, NM 87710 *505-377-6869*
Dean & Joan Douglass, Innkeepers
EMAIL *wildflower@angelfirenm.com*
WEBSITE *angelfirenm.com/wildflower*

LOCATION	Just under 2.5 miles south from the blinking light at the intersection of Highways 64 and 434; turn east onto Halo Pines Terrace and drive 0.5 mile.
OPEN	All year
DESCRIPTION	A 1996 two-story country host home decorated with country furnishings and antiques.
NO. OF ROOMS	Three rooms with private bathrooms and two rooms share one bathroom. Try the Wild Rose Room.
RATES	Thanksgiving through March, rates are $85-150 for a single or double with a private bathroom and $65-85 for a single or double with a shared bathroom. April to Thanksgiving, rates are $75-125 for a single or double with a private bathroom and $65-75 for a single or double with a shared bathroom. There is no minimum stay and cancellation requires 30 days' notice from Thanksgiving through March, seven days the rest of the year.
CREDIT CARDS	No
BREAKFAST	Full gourmet breakfast is served in the dining room and may include Swedish oatmeal pancakes, Swedish fruit soup, muffins, and homemade granola bars.

AMENITIES TV/VCR in all rooms, ceiling fans, electric blankets.

RESTRICTIONS No smoking, no pets, children of any age are welcome in the family suite. Children over 12 are welcome in the other rooms. Sweet Pea is the resident Yorkshire terrier.

ARROYO SECO

LAS CAMPANAS DE TAOS

41 State Road 230, Arroyo Seco, NM 87514 *505-776-5777*

ARTESIA

HERITAGE INN

209 West Main, Artesia, NM 88210 *505-748-2552*
FAX 505-746-3407

AZTEC

MISS GAIL'S INN

305 South Main, Aztec, NM 87401 *505-334-3452*
John & Gail Aspromonte, Resident Owners

BERNALILLO

(ALBUQUERQUE)

Just north of Albuquerque off I-25, Bernalillo once played host to Coronado for two years. From here, you are well positioned for trips to Santa Fe or Albuquerque.

LA HACIENDA GRANDE

21 Barros Lane, Bernalillo, NM 87004 — *505-867-1887*
Shoshana Zimmerman, Innkeeper — *800-353-1887*
Spanish spoken — *FAX 505-771-1436*
EMAIL lhg@swcp.com — *WEBSITE www.lahaciendagrande.com*

LOCATION	From Albuquerque, take I-25 north toward Santa Fe to exit 242. Turn left (west), and go past the Super 8 to the first stoplight. Turn right onto Camino Del Pueblo and drive north for approximately 0.5 mile. Turn left at the sign and go straight down the country lane to the inn.
OPEN	All year
DESCRIPTION	A 1745 Southwest adobe inn with beamed cathedral ceilings, decorated in warm earth tones with wrought iron and rattan furniture, leather-back chairs, and local New Mexican and Native American artwork. The inn features a central courtyard and a large, landscaped front yard.
NO. OF ROOMS	Six rooms with private bathrooms. Try the San Felipe Room.
RATES	Year-round rates are $99-139 for a single or double. There is no minimum stay and cancellation requires 11 days' notice with a $15 fee. "If guests cancel within 10 days or less of their expected arrival date, we issue them a transferable gift certificate for the entire stay redeemable for up to one year but we do charge the full amount of the reserved stay."
CREDIT CARDS	American Express, Diners Club, Discover, MasterCard, Visa
BREAKFAST	Full breakfast is served in the dining room and includes spinach and Gruyère cheese quiche, amaretto French toast, pumpkin walnut pancakes, or zucchini frittata. The main dishes are often accompanied by country potatoes, turkey bacon, or sausage. All breakfasts include fresh fruit, bread or muffins, orange juice, coffee, and tea. Lunch, dinner, and special meals (including diet, low fat, and vegetarian) are available upon request.
AMENITIES	Air-conditioned rooms, fireplaces, a guest telephone line, board games and books, CD player, TV/VCRs, hair dryers, irons and ironing boards, radio alarm clocks, "most frequently forgotten items" available upon request, wine and light snack upon arrival.

RESTRICTIONS	No pets
REVIEWED	*Country Inns* magazine
MEMBER	New Mexico Bed & Breakfast Association, Albuquerque Bed & Breakfast Association, Professional Association of Innkeepers International, Innkeepers Only, Greater Albuquerque Innkeepers Association
RATED	AAA 3 Diamonds, Mobil 3 Stars
AWARDS	1995, The Year's Top 24 Inns, *Country Inns* magazine; 1995, Top Inn Buys, *Country Inns* magazine

CANONCITO

APACHE CANYON RANCH B&B

4 Canyon Drive, Canoncito, NM 87026 — *505-836-7220*
WEBSITE www.apachecanyon.com

KUDOS/COMMENTS "Sophisticated isolation, yet with all the amenities."

CEDAR CREST

(ALBUQUERQUE)

Cedar Crest sits on the historic Turquoise Trail (Highway 14) up above Albuquerque, in the Sandia Mountains.

ELAINE'S, A BED & BREAKFAST

72 Snowline Estates, Cedar Crest, NM 87008 — *505-281-2467*
Elaine O'Neil, Resident Owner — *800-821-3092*
WEBSITE www.elainesbnb.com

LOCATION	From Albuquerque, take I-40 east to exit 175 toward Cedar Crest. Go 4 miles north and turn left at the Turquoise Trail Campground sign. Go straight on a dirt road approximately 0.5 mile and turn left at the T. Enter the gate marked "Snowline Estates" and find the B&B on the right.
OPEN	All year

DESCRIPTION	A 1979 three-story log and native stone home furnished with country antiques.
NO. OF ROOMS	Five rooms with private bathrooms.
RATES	Year-round rates for a single or double are $85-139. Ask about a minimum stay and cancellation policy.
CREDIT CARDS	American Express, Discover, MasterCard, Visa
BREAKFAST	Full breakfast is served.
AMENITIES	Two rooms with fireplaces and shared balconies and three with Jacuzzis and private balconies.
RESTRICTIONS	No smoking inside, no pets, children over five are welcome.
REVIEWED	*Fodor's Santa Fe, Taos, Albuquerque; Off the Beaten Path—New Mexico; America's Wonderful Little Hotels & Inns*
MEMBER	Professional Association of Innkeepers International
KUDOS/COMMENTS	"Nice people, beautiful place." "Charming, modern-rustic, very comfortable, homey breakfast and friendly." "Friendly hostess, nice three-story log home." (1996)

CERRILLOS

Half an hour south of Santa Fe on Highway 14, Cerrillos is well situated to offer easy access to the best of northern New Mexico. Explore Cerrillos Village, an old mining town and the movie set for Young Guns and other films, and don1t miss the Cerrillos Mining Museum. Madrid, an old coal-mining town and present-day artists1 colony, is just down the road; Waldo, a ghost town, lies 2 miles west of Cerrillos Village.

HEART SEED B&B AND SPA

County Road 55, Cerrillos, NM 87010 — *505-471-7026*
Judith Polich, Innkeeper — *FAX 505-471-8059*
EMAIL hrtseed@nets.com — *WEBSITE www.nets.com/heartseed*

LOCATION	From Santa Fe, take Highway 14 south. Go 0.25 mile past the exit to the village of Cerrillos and turn left onto County Road 55. Drive exactly 5 miles to the B&B.
OPEN	All year
DESCRIPTION	A 1990s two-story Santa Fe–style inn located on 70 high-desert acres in the Ontiz Mountains.
NO. OF ROOMS	Six rooms with private bathrooms.

RATES	Year-round rates are $79-89 for a single or double and $110-150 for one of two guesthouses. There is a minimum stay during high season in the guesthouses; cancellation requires two weeks' notice.
CREDIT CARDS	American Express, MasterCard, Visa
BREAKFAST	Full breakfast is served in the dining room Friday through Monday. Tuesday through Thursday, breakfast baskets are delivered to the rooms.
AMENITIES	Hot tub, hiking trails, meditation garden and labyrinth, evening snacks, full day spa.
RESTRICTIONS	No smoking, no pets. Bella is the resident pooch.
MEMBER	Professional Association of Innkeepers International

Old Boarding House

2885 State Highway 14 N, Cerrillos, NM 87010 *505-471-5134*

Chama

A railroad town with a depot for the famous Cumbres and Toltec Narrow Gauge Railroad, which runs from Memorial Day through October. Chama is a great spot for backcountry skiing. Take in the Chama Valley Music Festival in July. Located 10 miles from the Colorado border, northwest of Santa Fe and southeast of Durango.

Cardin's Crossing

551 Maple Avenue, Chama, NM 87520 *505-756-2542*
Tom & Mary Cardin, Resident Owners *800-852-6400*
Spanish spoken

LOCATION	One block west of Highway 17 (Terrace Avenue). Entering Old Town Chama from the south, turn left on 6th Street, go 1 block, and turn right on Maple.
OPEN	All year
DESCRIPTION	A 1995 cottage-style host home with gingerbread porches, gardens, and bird feeders. Decorated with country Victorian furnishings.
NO. OF ROOMS	Two rooms with private bathrooms.

RATES	Late May through mid-October, rates are $79-89 for a single or double. Late October through mid-May, rates are $65-75. There is no minimum stay and cancellation requires seven days' notice.
CREDIT CARDS	Discover, MasterCard, Visa
BREAKFAST	Continental plus is served in the dining room and includes fresh fruit compote, juices, Yankee porridge with cream and Vermont maple syrup, Alaska sourdough cinnamon rolls, and gourmet coffees. Box lunches are available.
AMENITIES	Homemade apple pie every evening, antique handmade quilts, meeting area, computer access, train reservations, G. Gauge model train in narrow gauge room, dollhouse and porcelain dolls, canopy bed, fresh flowers and candy in rooms.
RESTRICTIONS	No smoking, no pets, all children are welcome.

CASA DE MARINEZ

Old US 84, Los Brazos, NM 87551 *505-588-7858*
Clorinda & Medardo Sanchez, Resident Owners
Spanish spoken

LOCATION	Nine miles south of Chama off Highway 84, on County Road 334.
OPEN	February 15 through October 15
DESCRIPTION	A 1861–1912 two-story Southwest Victorian adobe decorated with antiques, southwestern furnishings, and Native American art. Listed on the State and National Historic Registers.
NO. OF ROOMS	Five rooms with private bathrooms.
RATES	May through October, rates are $80-115 for a single or double and $85-125 for a suite. There is no minimum stay and cancellation requires 10 days' notice with a $15 fee.
CREDIT CARDS	MasterCard, Visa
BREAKFAST	Full breakfast is served in the dining room and includes coffee, juices, fruit, pastries, granola, French toast, egg dishes, and chile dishes.
AMENITIES	Bath amenities, flowers, robes, hair dryers, and hors d'oeuvres.
RESTRICTIONS	No smoking inside, no pets, children over 13 are welcome.
REVIEWED	*Off the Beaten Path—New Mexico; America's Wonderful Little Hotels & Inns; American Adobes—Rural Houses of Northern New Mexico*
MEMBER	New Mexico Bed & Breakfast Association, Chama Valley Chamber of Commerce

RATED	AAA 3 Diamonds
KUDOS/COMMENTS	"Lovely historic family home, charming hosts, exceptional food, a hidden treasure of hispanic culture."

ENCHANTED DEER HAVEN B&B

PO Box 608, Chama, NM 87520 — *505-588-7535*
WEBSITE *www.bbhost.com/EnchantedDeerHaven* — *800-619-3337*

THE GANDY DANCER B&B INN

299 Maple Avenue, Chama, NM 87520 — *505-756-2191*
Darryl & Anita Dismuke, Resident Owners — *800-424-6702*
EMAIL *frontdesk@gandydancerbb.com* — *FAX 505-756-9110*
WEBSITE *www.gandydancerbb.com*

LOCATION	One block north of the train depot (Terrace Avenue), turn left on 3rd Street, and go 1 block to the corner of Maple and 3rd.
OPEN	All year
DESCRIPTION	A 1912 two-story Victorian decorated with antiques and contemporary art.
NO. OF ROOMS	Seven rooms with private bathrooms.
RATES	May through October, the rate for a single or double is $95. November through April, a single or double is $75. There is no minimum stay and cancellation requires seven days' notice.
CREDIT CARDS	American Express, Discover, MasterCard, Visa
BREAKFAST	Full gourmet breakfast is served in the dining room. Lunch and dinner is available by reservation.
AMENITIES	Hot tub; outdoor fire pit; coffee, tea, cocoa bar; guest refrigerator; fruit bowl.
RESTRICTIONS	No smoking, no pets, children over 12 are welcome.
RATED	AAA 3 Diamonds

The Parlor Car Bed & Breakfast

311 Terrace Avenue, Chama, NM 87520 — *505-756-1946*
Wendy & Bonsall Johnson, Innkeepers — *888-849-7800*
"Broken" Spanish spoken

LOCATION	On the corner of 3rd and Terrace Avenue (Highway 17).
OPEN	All year
DESCRIPTION	A 1928 two-story Tudor-style adobe host home, built by Chama's first banker, with bay windows and original pressed-tin ceilings.
NO. OF ROOMS	Three rooms with private bathrooms. Wendy recommends the Pullman Room, with a two-person whirlpool tub.
RATES	Mid-May to mid-October, rates are $65-90 for a single or double. Mid-October to mid-May, rates are $50-70 for a single or double. There is no minimum stay. Discounts for stays of four nights or more. Cancellation requires seven days' notice for a full refund.
CREDIT CARDS	American Express, Carte Blanche, Diners Club, Discover, JCB, MasterCard, Visa
BREAKFAST	Full breakfast is served in the dining room and includes coffee, tea, hot chocolate, orange juice, a fruit dish, breads (muffins, scones, coffeecake), and a main dish with meat, eggs, cheese, and vegetables. Box lunches are available for train rides, fishing, hiking, or sightseeing outings.
AMENITIES	Cookies and cool water in the rooms, piano in living room, book and video libraries, garden area with glider, Adirondack chairs, downstairs room is handicapped accessible, bird-watching, candies, original oil paintings, luxury bedding and towels.
RESTRICTIONS	No smoking, well-behaved children are welcome.

Chimayo

On the high road (Highway 76) to Taos, 30 miles north of Santa Fe, Chimayo has been a weaving center since the 1880s. The Sanctuario de Chimayo draws thousands of visitors on Good Friday and during holy week.

Casa Escondida

Route 0100, Chimayo, NM 87522 — *505-351-4805*
Irenka Taurek, Resident Owner — *800-643-7201*
German, Russian, and Polish spoken — *FAX 505-351-2575*

LOCATION	From Highway 76, on the road to Taos, take County Road 0100 for 0.25 mile.
OPEN	All year
DESCRIPTION	A 1968 two-story northern New Mexico adobe furnished with Mission period pieces, situated on 6 acres.
NO. OF ROOMS	Eight rooms with private bathrooms. One room has a private bathroom in the hallway.
RATES	Year-round rates for a single or double are $75-130. There is no minimum stay and cancellation requires 10 days' notice.
CREDIT CARDS	American Express, MasterCard, Visa
BREAKFAST	Full breakfast is served in the dining room and includes fresh-squeezed orange juice, fruit plate, French toast, turkey ham, and coffee.
AMENITIES	Hot tub; robes; sherry, port, and cookies; afternoon tea is available; lemonade is available in the summer.
RESTRICTIONS	No smoking. The resident dogs are Pinta and Polly.
REVIEWED	*Fodor's Southwest; The Non-Smokers Guide to Bed & Breakfasts*
MEMBER	New Mexico Bed & Breakfast Association

HACIENDA RANCHO DE CHIMAYO

County Road 98, Chimayo, NM 87522 — *505-351-2222*
Florence Jaramillo, Innkeeper — *FAX 505-351-2222*
Spanish spoken

LOCATION	From Santa Fe, take Highway 84/285 north for 16 miles. Go past the Cities of Gold Casino in Pojoaque to the stoplight at State Route 503. Turn right and drive 7.5 miles to County Road 98. Turn left and go 3 miles to the driveway on the left, across the street from Rancho de Chimayo restaurant.
OPEN	All year
DESCRIPTION	A restored 1800s-era territorial country inn decorated with period antiques and rooms that open onto a courtyard.
NO. OF ROOMS	Seven rooms with private bathrooms.
RATES	April through October and holidays, rates are $69-105 for a double. November through March, rates are $52-79 for a double. There is no minimum stay and cancellation requires 10 days' written notice.
CREDIT CARDS	American Express, Discover, MasterCard, Visa

BREAKFAST	Continental breakfast is served in the guestrooms or on the patio or courtyard and includes juice or fruit, coffee, tea, cocoa, and pastry that varies daily.
RESTRICTIONS	No smoking, no pets, children over 10 are welcome. There is a resident cat.
MEMBER	New Mexico Hotel and Motel Association

La Posada de Chimayo

279 Rio Arriba County Road 0101, Chimayo, NM 87522 *505-351-4605*
Spanish spoken *FAX 505-351-4605*

LOCATION	Drive 8 miles east of Espanola on Route 76. Turn north on Rio Arriba County Road 88 (turns into 0101); always stay to the right—make no left turns. The inn is on the left, a little over a mile from Route 76.
OPEN	All year
DESCRIPTION	A pitched-roof, traditional adobe farmhouse and guesthouse on a backroad in a decidedly rural neighborhood. Decorated with southwestern furnishings.
NO. OF ROOMS	Four rooms with private bathrooms.
RATES	Please inquire about current rates and cancellation information.
CREDIT CARDS	No
BREAKFAST	Full breakfast is served in the dining room.
AMENITIES	Fireplaces in all rooms, guests may help themselves to wine.
RESTRICTIONS	Smoking outside only, no pets without prior approval.
REVIEWED	*America's Wonderful Little Hotels & Inns; Fodor's New Mexico; Bed & Breakfast Guide—Southwest: Arizona, New Mexico, Texas; Best Places to Stay in the Southwest*
MEMBER	New Mexico Bed & Breakfast Association, Professional Association of Innkeepers International

Rancho Manzana

26 Camino de Mision, Chimayo, NM 87522 — *505-351-2227*
Jody Apple, Resident Owner — *888-505-2227*
Spanish spoken — *FAX 505-351-2223*
EMAIL manzana@newmexico.com — *WEBSITE www.taoswebb.com/manzana*

LOCATION	Drive 13 miles north of Santa Fe on Highway 84/285. Take State Road 503, 10 miles to County Road 98, turn and go 4 miles. Turn left on County Road 94E, drive 0.25 mile and turn left into the driveway.
OPEN	All year
DESCRIPTION	A 1750s-era two-story territorial adobe that was the family residence and mercantile of the Vista Ortega family; decorated in eclectic New Mexican folk and country furnishings.
NO. OF ROOMS	Two rooms with private bathrooms and two cottages with private bathrooms.
RATES	June through October and holidays, rates are $97-112 for a single or double. November through May, a single or double is $85. There is no minimum stay and cancellation requires seven days' notice.
CREDIT CARDS	MasterCard, Visa
BREAKFAST	Full breakfast is served in the dining room or outdoors under the grape arbor and includes freshly squeezed orange juice, fresh fruit, omelets, frittatas, pancakes, and homemade breads.
AMENITIES	Outdoor sitting areas, pond, hot tub and fire pit, robes, down comforters, fireplaces in the main house, cooking school offering classes in regional and gourmet cuisine.
RESTRICTIONS	No smoking, no pets, children over 10 are welcome.
REVIEWED	*West* magazine, *Travel & Leisure*
MEMBER	Professional Association of Innkeepers International
AWARDS	May 1995, Best Places to Eat and Sleep in the World, Metropolitan Home

Cimarron

Cimarron sits on one of the more beautiful drives in the world: Highway 64, from Taos to just south of Raton. The town is adjacent to the Philmont Scout Ranch and the Santa Fe Trail.

Casa del Gavilan

Highway 21 South, Cimarron, NM 87714 — *505-376-2246*
FAX 505-376-2247

LOCATION	Six miles south of Cimarron on Highway 21.
OPEN	All year
DESCRIPTION	A 1906 adobe villa nestled in the foothills of the Sangre de Cristo Mountains.
NO. OF ROOMS	Five rooms with private bathrooms.
RATES	Please inquire about current rates and cancellation information.
CREDIT CARDS	American Express, MasterCard, Visa
BREAKFAST	Full breakfast is served in the dining room and includes quiche, pancakes, or French toast, bread or muffins, and fruit.
AMENITIES	Handicapped accessible.
RESTRICTIONS	No smoking inside, no pets
MEMBER	American Bed & Breakfast Association, Professional Association of Innkeepers International

Cloudcroft

Twenty miles east of Alamogordo on Highway 82, Cloudcroft is perched at just under 9,000 feet in the Sacramento Mountains. Enjoy Christmas in the Clouds and the Labor Day Fiesta.

The Crofting B&B

300 Swallow Place, Cloudcroft, NM 88317 — *505-682-2288*
Lee Wilson, Resident Owner
EMAIL *lee@zianet.com*

LOCATION	Highway 82 runs through town; turn south on Swallow Place, and go two-and-a-half blocks. There is a sign on the left.
OPEN	All year
DESCRIPTION	A circa 1915 two-story log country inn with red and white trim and antique furnishings.
NO. OF ROOMS	Eight rooms with private bathrooms.
RATES	Year-round rates for a single or double are $79-85 and the suite is $125. There is no minimum stay and cancellation requires seven days' notice.
CREDIT CARDS	American Express, Discover, MasterCard, Visa
BREAKFAST	Continental breakfast is served in the family kitchen.
AMENITIES	Balcony off each room, wet bar with microwave and coffee-maker, cable TV with HBO, queen beds in all rooms, pool table, kitchen privileges, Great Room with fireplace.
RESTRICTIONS	Smoking only in the game room, no children under 14 please. The resident yellow Lab is called Honey.
KUDOS/COMMENTS	"Friendly host. Very well decorated. Convenient to town." (1999)

LAS BANDERAS

680 Cox Canyon, Cloudcroft, NM 88317 — *505-682-2952*
Velia & Thomas Perea, Resident Owners

BURRO STREET BOARDING HOUSE

608 Burro Avenue, Cloudcroft, NM 88317 — *505-682-3601*
Linda Carter, Innkeeper — *888-682-3601*
EMAIL *lindalc@zianet.com* — *FAX 505-682-3601*

LOCATION	Burro Avenue is the main street in Cloudcroft. The boarding house is a half block east of the shops on the boardwalk.
OPEN	All year
DESCRIPTION	A 1995 two-story log home furnished with comfortable country antiques, wood stove, and decks overlooking the charming town of Cloudcroft.
NO. OF ROOMS	Three rooms with private bathrooms. Linda likes the Loft.

RATES	Year-round rate for a single or double is $68. The log cabin is $110. There is no minimum stay and cancellation requires 14 days' notice.
CREDIT CARDS	MasterCard, Visa
BREAKFAST	Full breakfast is served in the dining room and includes juice, coffee, green-chile casserole, banana bread, fresh fruit, homemade jams, jellies, and picante.
AMENITIES	Handicapped accessible, champagne for anniversaries, snowshoes, sleds.
RESTRICTIONS	No smoking, no pets
MEMBER	International Bed & Breakfast Association

The Pavilion at the Lodge

1 Corona Place, Cloudcroft, NM 88317 — *505-682-2566*
EMAIL *thelodge-nm@zianet.com* — *800-395-6343*
FAX 505-682-2715

Columbus

Things have calmed down here since Poncho Villa raided and burned the town in 1916. Columbus kicks up its heels the second week in October during the Columbus Festival. Three miles from the Mexican border and 32 miles south of Demming, on Highway 11.

Helen's Hide-Away B & B

Sunshine Way in the City of the Sun, Columbus, NM 88029 — *505-531-2691*
Helen Webber, Innkeeper
Spanish spoken

LOCATION	Take Highway 11 south from Deming to the Columbus City limits. Turn west at the yellow City of the Sun sign onto Altura Street, go 2 blocks, turn right at the smaller City of the Sun sign. Go 2 blocks to Sunshine Way and turn left.
OPEN	All year
DESCRIPTION	A 1990 stabilized adobe with Southwest decor.

NO. OF ROOMS	Two rooms with private bathrooms.
RATES	Year-round rates are $22 for a single or double. There is no minimum stay requirement.
CREDIT CARDS	No
BREAKFAST	Continental breakfast is served and includes juice, coffee, homemade muffins, cereal, and milk.
AMENITIES	Hot tub and spa facilities, RV hookup, native cactus gardens.
RESTRICTIONS	No pets

Martha's Place

---

32 Lima Street, Columbus, NM 88029 — *505-531-2467*
Martha Skinner, Resident Owner — *FAX 505-531-2479*
EMAIL *marthas@vtc.net*

LOCATION	Two blocks west of Highway 11 on Lima Street.
OPEN	All year
DESCRIPTION	A 1991 two-story territorial with country furnishings.
NO. OF ROOMS	Five rooms with private bathrooms.
RATES	Year-round rates for a single or double are $50-65. There is no minimum stay and cancellation requires 24 hours' notice.
CREDIT CARDS	MasterCard, Visa
BREAKFAST	Full breakfast is served in the dining room and includes juice, fruit, egg dish, meat, coffee, and breakfast rolls or cake.
AMENITIES	Air conditioning, theater in season, assistance with crossing into Mexico and transportation.
RESTRICTIONS	None
REVIEWED	*Hidden Southwest*

COOLIDGE

Twenty miles east of Gallup on I-40, Coolidge is close to Navajo, Zuni, and Acoma reservations and Chaco Canyon.

STAUDER'S NAVAJO LODGE BED & BREAKFAST

HC 32 Box 1, Coolidge, NM 87312 *505-862-7553*
Sherwood & Roberta Stauder, Resident Owners

LOCATION	From Gallup, go east 20 miles on I-40. Take exit 44 to West Coolidge Road.
OPEN	March 1 through October 31 (but open during the winter for the Crown Point Rug Auction)
DESCRIPTION	A remodeled early 1930s ranch-style Spanish hacienda furnished with antiques and Native American and Mexican arts and crafts.
NO. OF ROOMS	Two rooms with private bathrooms.
RATES	Year-round rates for a single or double are $89-125. There is no minimum stay and cancellation requires 48 hours' notice, seven days during auction dates and Intertribal Ceremonial.
CREDIT CARDS	American Express, MasterCard, Visa (prefer checks)
BREAKFAST	Continental plus is served in the dining room or the Great Room in the main residence and includes coffee, tea, fruit, hotcakes, or casserole.
AMENITIES	Flowers, welcome baskets, and daily treats.
RESTRICTIONS	No smoking, no pets, Buster is the resident Australian shepherd and Socks and Emmy are the cats. There are also three horses, and a llama named Valentino. The horses love to run and play with sticks and garden hoses.

CORRALES

Settled in the 1700s, Corrales retains its own distinct, rustic character, even as Albuquerque threatens to swallow it up. Casa San Ysidro, Petroglyph National Park, and Acoma Pueblo are all nearby.

THE CHOCOLATE TURTLE B&B

1098 West Meadowlark Lane, Corrales, NM 87048 — *505-898-1800*
Carole Morgan, Resident Owner — *800-898-1842*
EMAIL turtlebb@aol.com — *FAX 505-898-5328*
WEBSITE www.collectorsguide.com/chocturtle

LOCATION	Drive north on I-25 from the Albuquerque airport to Paseo del Norte. Exit to Coors Road and drive two miles to Corrales Road. Go 1.5 miles on Corrales Road to Meadowlark, go left on Meadowlark for 1 mile, and turn right into the driveway.
OPEN	All year
DESCRIPTION	A 1979 territorial-style home on 1.5 acres. The house is decorated with southwestern furnishings and has a patio with views of the Sandia Mountains and city lights.
NO. OF ROOMS	Four rooms with private bathrooms.
RATES	Year-round rates for a single or double are $60-100. Discounts are available for multiple-night stays; a minimum stay is required during the Balloon Fiesta and cancellation requires seven days' notice.
CREDIT CARDS	American Express, Discover, MasterCard, Visa
BREAKFAST	Full breakfast is served in the dining room and changes all the time, but fruit is always included.
AMENITIES	Hot tub, guest refrigerator stocked with cold drinks, snacks at night, chocolate turtles, specialty soaps, kettle for hot drinks in the dining room, microwave and dishes, guest phone, romance packages available.
RESTRICTIONS	No smoking, no pets, children over five are welcome.
REVIEWED	*America's Wonderful Little Hotels & Inns; Recommended Country Inns—The Southwest*
RATED	AAA 3 Diamonds, Mobil 3 Stars
KUDOS/COMMENTS	"New, great chocolate turtles." (1996)

Corrales Inn Bed & Breakfast

58 Perea Road, Corrales, NM 87048 — *505-897-4422*
Ron & Pat Moffat, Resident Owners — *800-897-4410*
Spanish spoken — *FAX 505-890-5244 (call first)*
EMAIL info@corralesinn.com — *WEBSITE www.corralesinn.com*

LOCATION	From I-25 take exit 233 (Alameda Boulevard) west, cross over the Rio Grande and take the first right on Corrales Road. Go 2.9 miles to Corrales Elementary School and go left on Perea Road.
OPEN	All year
DESCRIPTION	A 1986 pueblo-style inn with southwestern, Santa Fe–style furnishings and Native American and cowboy art, antiques, and collectibles.
NO. OF ROOMS	Six rooms with private bathrooms. Ron suggests the Corrales Room.
RATES	Year-round rates for a single or double are $65-95. There is a minimum stay during the Balloon Fiesta in early October and cancellation requires 10 days' notice with a $20 fee.
CREDIT CARDS	American Express, MasterCard, Visa
BREAKFAST	Full gourmet breakfast is served in the dining room and includes smoothie fruit drinks, fresh fruit, a wide variety of egg dishes, pancakes, French toast, quiches, and stratas. "Stay two weeks and you'll never get the same breakfast twice," says Ron.
AMENITIES	Two-thousand-volume library with regional travel and art books, 24-hour coffee and tea station in living room, courtyard with hummingbirds, fireplaces, individual heating and air conditioning, and nature walks along the Rio Grande.
RESTRICTIONS	No smoking, no pets. The resident parrot, called Groucho, speaks Spanish and allegedly sings "La Cucaracha." The Italian greyhound is called Blue Baby.
REVIEWED	*Journey to the High Southwest; Fodor's Santa Fe, Taos, & Albuquerque; The Insider's Guide to Santa Fe; Off the Beaten Path—New Mexico; America's Wonderful Little Hotels & Inns; Recommended Country Inns—The Southwest*
MEMBER	Albuquerque Bed & Breakfast Association
KUDOS/COMMENTS	"Lovely, quiet and peaceful, well-kept B&B with charming innkeepers." "New owners, clean, new decor." (1996)

La Mimosa Bed & Breakfast

1144 Andrews Lane, Corrales, NM 87048 — *505-898-1354*
Glorya Mueller, Resident Owner — *FAX 505-898-0635*
Some German spoken
EMAIL Lamimosbb@aol.com

LOCATION From the intersection of Corrales Road and Alameda, go 2.4 miles north on Corrales Road to East Ella. Go right on East Ella 0.1 mile to a ditch, cross the ditch, and take an immediate left onto the dirt road. Go 0.2 mile to the driveway.

OPEN All year

DESCRIPTION An adobe guesthouse decorated with Navajo rugs, original art, and Mexican pots.

NO. OF ROOMS One guesthouse with a sitting area and sleeping area.

RATES Year-round rates are $50 for a single and $65 for a double. There is a minimum stay on weekends. Ask about a cancellation policy.

CREDIT CARDS No

BREAKFAST Continental breakfast is served in the guesthouse or in the garden and includes fresh-squeezed orange juice, coffee or tea, a fresh fruit course, warm muffins and homemade bread with sweet butter, jams, honey, and a platter of cheese and grapes. Special dietary needs are accommodated.

AMENITIES Fresh flowers; fruit basket, wine; coffee-maker with an assortment of tea, coffee, and cocoa in the kitchen; CD player; heat and air conditioning; wicker seating areas; hammock and barbecues in walled garden; numerous walking paths and Rio Grande; outdoor fireplace for stargazing on chilly evenings.

RESTRICTIONS No smoking, please call about pets ("depends on size and disposition"). Children over 12 are welcome.

REVIEWED *Hidden Southwest; America's Wonderful Little Hotels & Inns; Wake Up and Smell the Coffee*

Nora Dixon Place

312 Dixon Road, Corrales, NM 87048 — *505-898-3662*

SANDHILL CRANE BED & BREAKFAST

389 Camino Hermosa, Corrales, NM 87048 *505-898-2445*
Margo MacInnes, Innkeeper *800-375-2445*
FAX 505-898-1189

LOCATION	Take exit 233 (Alameda Boulevard) off I-25 and drive 4.25 miles west to Corrales Road. Turn right and drive 3.25 miles. Just past San Ysidro Church, take a left onto Camino Hermosa (also called Tenorio Road). The B&B is on the left just past the intersection with Loma Largo Road.
OPEN	All year
DESCRIPTION	A rambling adobe hacienda furnished with antiques and international folk art, with timbered ceilings and brick floors. The country inn is nestled amongst towering pines with landscaped courtyards.
NO. OF ROOMS	Two rooms with private bathrooms and two rooms share one bathroom. Try the Meadow Room, with a queen-size bed and private patio and entrance.
RATES	Year-round rates are $90 for a single or double with a private bathroom, $80 for a single or double with a shared bathroom, and $160 for a suite. There is a minimum stay during holidays and special events and cancellation requires 48 hours' notice.
CREDIT CARDS	American Express, MasterCard, Visa
BREAKFAST	Full breakfast is served in the dining room or on the outdoor terrace and includes juice, fresh fruit in season, muffins, waffles, egg casseroles, scones, bacon or ham, fresh-ground coffee, and herbal or breakfast teas.
AMENITIES	Fresh flowers throughout, hot tub, facilities for small meetings, hot-air balloon rides, in-room refrigerators.
RESTRICTIONS	No smoking, no pets, children over six are welcome. Jazz is the resident cat.
MEMBER	New Mexico Bed & Breakfast Association, Albuquerque Bed & Breakfast Association
RATED	AAA 3 Diamonds

VISTA HERMOSA LLAMA FARM BED & BREAKFAST

475 Camino de Corrales Del Norte, Corrales, NM 87048 *505-898-0864*

Yours Truly Bed & Breakfast

160 Paseo de Corrales, Corrales, NM 87048 — *505-898-7027*
Pat & James Montgomery, Innkeepers — *800-942-7890*
Texan spoken — *FAX 505-898-9022*
EMAIL yourstrulybb@juno.com — *WEBSITE www.yourstrulybb.com*

LOCATION	From Albuquerque, go north on I-25, then west 4.3 miles on Alameda Boulevard across the Rio Grande to the second stoplight at Corrales Road. Turn right (north) and go 1.7 miles. Turn left (west) onto Meadowlark, continue 1 mile, and turn right onto Loma Largo. Take a left at the second road and follow Paseo de Corrales to the third house on the right.
OPEN	All year
DESCRIPTION	A 1982 Southwest adobe host home with brick floors, whimsical southwestern decor, and fantastic views of city lights, mountains, and valleys.
NO. OF ROOMS	Four rooms with private bathrooms.
RATES	Year-round rates are $89-110 for a single or double. There is no minimum stay and cancellation requires 24 hours' notice with a $25 fee.
CREDIT CARDS	American Express, Diners Club, Discover, MasterCard, Visa
BREAKFAST	Full breakfast is served in the dining room or on the patio, or is delivered to guestrooms. Breakfast includes coffee, juice, fresh fruit platter, fruit bread, and a hot entrée such as biscuits with sausage and green-chile gravy, praline French toast, or breakfast enchiladas.
AMENITIES	Candy and fruit any time; flowers in rooms and on breakfast trays; napkins printed with guests' names; robes; beer and wine any time; happy hour; sodas; loaner bikes and coolers; maps; guests can crew and photo shoot with hot air balloon (passengers pay extra); air-conditioned rooms; each room has extra pillows and throws; king-size beds; fireplaces; hot tub.
RESTRICTIONS	None. Children over six are welcome. Whack is the resident Manx cat and Meep-Meep is the roadrunner.
REVIEWED	*Fodor's; Southwest Four Corners; Art of Visiting Albuquerque*
MEMBER	New Mexico Bed & Breakfast Association, Albuquerque Bed & Breakfast Association
RATED	AAA 3 Diamonds

COSTILLA

COSTILLA BED & BREAKFAST

PO Box 125, Costilla, NM 87524 *505-586-1683*
FAX 505-586-1352

DIXON

During the first weekend of November, this sleepy little village plays host to a couple thousand flatlanders for the Studio Tour. Designate a driver and then drop in on La Chiripada Winery. Dixon is a little over halfway between Santa Fe and Taos, on scenic Highway 68.

LA CASITA GUESTHOUSE

Highway 75, #16 Road #1119, Dixon, NM 87527 *505-579-4297*
Sara Pene & Celeste Miller, Resident Owners
Spanish spoken

LOCATION	Go 0.2 mile past the post office to the second road on the left at the La Chiripada Winery sign, Road #1119.
OPEN	All year
DESCRIPTION	A 1985 two-bedroom adobe guesthouse with southwestern furnishings.
NO. OF ROOMS	Two rooms share one bathroom.
RATES	Year-round rates for a single or double are $75-115. There is a two-night minimum stay and cancellation requires 14 days' notice.
CREDIT CARDS	No
BREAKFAST	Continental plus is served in the dining room and includes yogurt, fruit, granola, milk, coffee, juice, homemade breads, and tea.
AMENITIES	Winery next door, flowers, bird-watching, weavery, cable TV/VCR, fireplace, garden patio.
RESTRICTIONS	No smoking inside, no pets, the resident dogs are Bonhu and Sadie and the cats are Cinnamon and Poppy.
KUDOS/COMMENTS	"Charming adobe guesthouse nestled between colorful gardens and vineyard. Gracious hosts Celeste & Sara treat their guests as friends." (1996)

Rock Pool Gardens

PO Box 208, Dixon, NM 87527 *505-579-4602*
Holly Haas & Will DeMaret, Resident Owners
Spanish and French spoken

LOCATION	Between Santa Fe and Taos on Highway 75, 2.5 miles off the Taos Highway across from La Chiripada Winery.
OPEN	All year
DESCRIPTION	A 1950s adobe with a two-room suite decorated with faux-painted walls, ceramic tile, and wood floors.
NO. OF ROOMS	Two room suite with two queen-size beds and a private bathroom.
RATES	Year-round rates are $80 for two people, $10 per night for each additional person. There is a two-night minimum stay and cancellation requires 10 days' notice.
CREDIT CARDS	No
BREAKFAST	Continental breakfast self-served from a partially stocked fridge that includes coffee, tea, and seasonal fruit.
AMENITIES	Enclosed, heated, all rock, indoor swimming pool and outdoor hot tub under the trees, handicapped accessible, hiking in the surrounding hills, and artist tours and studio available for use.
RESTRICTIONS	No smoking inside

Eagle Nest

Thirty-two miles northeast of Taos on beautiful Highway 64, midway between Angel Fire and Red River. Eagle Nest Lake features excellent trout and salmon fishing. Come in July for the Wings over Angel Fire Balloon Festival.

Two Eagles Bed & Breakfast

On Highway 38 North, Eagle Nest, NM 87718 *505-377-2991*
FAX 505-377-6620

LOCATION	Seven-and-a-half miles north of Eagle Nest on Highway 38 north, on the left side of the road.
OPEN	All year
DESCRIPTION	A 1986 three-story lodge located on a 36,000-acre ranch.

NO. OF ROOMS	Four rooms with private bathrooms and two rooms share one bathroom.
RATES	Year-round rates for a single or double with a private bathroom are \$110-150 and a single or a double with a shared bathroom is \$90. There is no minimum stay. Ask about a cancellation policy.
CREDIT CARDS	American Express, Discover, MasterCard, Visa
BREAKFAST	Full country breakfast is served in the dining room.
AMENITIES	Hot tub, satellite TV in each room, fireplaces in kitchen and front room, air hockey, pool table, exercise equipment.
RESTRICTIONS	No smoking, no pets. Children are welcome. Children under five stay free.

Española

Surrounded by the eight northern pueblos, Española lies in the fertile Española Valley, 25 miles north of Santa Fe on Highway 285. Nearby pueblos include Nanbe, Pojoaque, San Juan, San Ildefonso, and Santa Clara.

Casa del Rio

PO Box 92, Española, NM 87532 *505-753-2035*
Eileen & Mel Vigil, Resident Owners
WEBSITE www.fourcorners.com/nm/inns/casadelrio

KUDOS/COMMENTS "Excellent." "Good B&B." (1996)

Casa del Rio, Española

Inn at the Delta

304 Paseo de Onate NW, Española, NM 87532 — *505-753-9466*
Anthony Garcia, Resident Owner — *800-995-8599*
WEBSITE *www.newmexico.com/delta/deltahome.htm*

Inn of la Mesilla

Route 1, Box 368A, Española, NM 87532 — *505-753-5368*
Yolanda (Landy) Hoemann, Resident Owner — *888-276-7703*
Spanish spoken — *FAX 505-753-5368 (call first)*
WEBSITE *www.lamesilla.com*

LOCATION	The inn is 3 miles south of Española in the Valley of the Black Mesa, on Highway 399.
OPEN	All year
DESCRIPTION	A 1990 pueblo-style host home with southwestern decor and breathtaking views of the Black Mesa and Jemez Mountains.
NO. OF ROOMS	Two rooms with private bathrooms. Try the Green Room.
RATES	Year-round rate for a single or double is $90. There is a minimum stay on holidays and during the Indian Market. Cancellation requires 14 days' notice.
CREDIT CARDS	No
BREAKFAST	Full breakfast is served in the dining room and includes orange juice, coffee, tea, cereal, eggs and bacon, toast, tamales, beans, coffeecakes, muffins. Special meals are also available during holidays for an additional $10 per person.
AMENITIES	Flowers, robes, hot tub on the deck with incredible views, afternoon wine and hors d'oeuvres, Great Room with baby grand piano and fireplace.
RESTRICTIONS	No smoking, no pets (kennel close by), children over 14 are welcome. Watch out for the English springer spaniels, Pork Chop and particularly Te Bon, who "will goose some guests at no extra charge."
REVIEWED	*Bed & Breakfast Worldwide; The Official Bed & Breakfast Guide*

Ranchito San Pedro

76A, Highway 581, Española, NM 87532 — *505-753-0583*
Jan Hart, Innkeeper — *FAX 505-753-0600*
Spanish (un poco) spoken
EMAIL j-hart@roadrunner.com
WEBSITE www.bookgrrls.com/jan/bedbreak.htm

LOCATION — Just 1 mile south of Española driving north on Highway 84 from Santa Fe. Turn west (left) onto Highway 399 (La Mesilla Road) at the stoplight, drive 1 mile, turn north (right) onto Highway 581, and drive 0.7 mile to the sign.

OPEN — All year

DESCRIPTION — A 1993 pueblo-style stucco lodge decorated with modern furnishings with northern New Mexico accents. A former turkey ranch turned artist's home and gallery.

NO. OF ROOMS — Two rooms share one bathroom. Try the sunny South Room.

RATES — Year-round rates are $45-65 for a single or double and $200 for the guesthouse. There is no minimum stay.

CREDIT CARDS — Visa

BREAKFAST — Continental plus is served in the kitchen and includes coffee, tea, orange juice, fruit, bagels or toast with homemade jam, cream cheese, and often a local treat.

AMENITIES — Racing pigeons and other birds, studio/gallery/curio shop, guests are welcome to use the studio, garlic field, flowers, outdoor chairs and benches, iced or hot tea.

RESTRICTIONS — No smoking inside, children and pets are negotiable. Ged is the resident three-legged cat, and there are two parrots. "The conures (parrots) are learning to talk and like interacting."

Rancho de San Juan

Highway 285 at Milepost 340, Fairview, NM 87533 — *505-753-6818*
David Heath & John Johnson, Innkeepers — *FAX 505-753-6818*
Spanish spoken
EMAIL ranchosj@roadrunner.com
WEBSITE www.ranchodesanjuan.com

LOCATION — On Highway 285, 7 miles north of San Juan Pueblo between Española and Ojo Caliente.

OPEN — All year

DESCRIPTION	A 1994 southwestern country inn featuring expansive views of the Jemez Mountains, the Ojo Caliente River valley, and the magnificent rock formations and foothills of Georgia O'Keeffe country.
NO. OF ROOMS	Fourteen rooms with private bathrooms.
RATES	Year-round rates are $175-500 for a single or double. There is a minimum stay during holidays and cancellation requires 30 days' notice.
CREDIT CARDS	American Express, Discover, MasterCard, Visa
BREAKFAST	Full breakfast includes homemade granola or assorted cereals and a choice of entrée du jour.
AMENITIES	Sherry for two in rooms, terrycloth robes, Mobil four-star restaurant, hot tub, extraordinary views from all rooms, hiking trails.
RESTRICTIONS	No smoking, children over 12 are welcome. Rusty is the resident pooch.
REVIEWED	*Country Inns* magazine; *Best Places to Stay in the Southwest; America's Favorite Inns, B&Bs and Small Hotels; Fodor's; Elegant Small Hotels; Fodor's Southwest*
MEMBER	Relais et Chateau
RATED	Mobil 4 Stars (received award for both inn and restaurant)
KUDOS/COMMENTS	"Wonderful, elegant, fit for royalty. Best food ever." "Very elegant, well-appointed inn situated on many acres of beautiful New Mexico landscape. Excellent breakfasts and dinners. John and David are gracious innkeepers." (1996)

FARMINGTON

Orchards, farms, and coal mines make Farmington, on scenic Highway 64, the major industrial center of the Four Corners region. Enjoy the Apple Blossom Festival in April, Riverfest and Balloon Festival on Memorial Day, and the summer-long Anasazi Pageant. Four major Indian ruins lie within 60 miles, including Aztec Ruins National Monument, 15 miles to the northeast, and Chaco Canyon National Park, an easy drive south on Highway 371. The nearby San Juan River features world-class trout fishing.

CASA BLANCA INN

505 East La Plata Street, Farmington, NM 87401 — *505-327-6503*
Jim & Mary Fabian, Resident Managers — *FAX 505-326-5680*
WEBSITE www.farmington-nm-lodging.com

LOCATION	From Highway 64, turn on Butler, go 3 blocks, and turn west on La Plata Street. The inn is 1 block on the left.
OPEN	All year
DESCRIPTION	A 1954 two-story Spanish inn with eclectic furnishings, located on an acre of gardens overlooking the city.
NO. OF ROOMS	Six rooms with private bathrooms. The best room is the Sequito Suite.
RATES	Please inquire about current rates and cancellation information.
CREDIT CARDS	American Express, Discover, MasterCard, Visa
BREAKFAST	Full gourmet breakfast is served in bed or in the gardens. Lunch, dinner, and special low-fat meals are available.
AMENITIES	Nightly turndown service, afternoon tea, airport pick-up, cable TV/VCRs in rooms, robes, fresh flowers, and air conditioning.
RESTRICTIONS	No smoking, no pets, children over 12 are welcome.
KUDOS/COMMENTS	"Extremely well-run, large home, luxuriously furnished, well-kept lawn." (1996)

KOKOPELLI'S CAVE BED & BREAKFAST

206 West 38th Street, Farmington, NM 87401 — *505-325-7855*
Bruce Black, Innkeeper — *FAX 505-325-9671*
EMAIL *koko@cyberport.com* — WEBSITE *www.bbonline.com/nm/kokopelli*

LOCATION	From the intersection of Broadway Street and Butler, go north on Butler for 1.5 miles to 38th Street. Turn left and go to the end of the street.
OPEN	March through November
DESCRIPTION	A 1,650-square-foot home built into a vertical cliff face 250 feet above the La Plata River valley, decorated with an Anasazi motif, with plush carpeted living areas.
NO. OF ROOMS	One bedroom with a private bathroom.
RATES	Year-round rates are $175 for a double and $35 for each additional guest up to four. There is no minimum stay and cancellation requires one week's notice.
CREDIT CARDS	American Express, MasterCard, Visa
BREAKFAST	Serve-yourself continental breakfast includes cereal, milk, juice, rolls, coffee, and fruit. Special meals can be arranged with an additional charge.

AMENITIES	Wine coolers, fireplace, Kiva Room, waterfall shower and hot tub.
RESTRICTIONS	No smoking, no pets, children over 12 are welcome. There is abundant wildlife on the property.
REVIEWED	*Frommer's New Mexico*

Silver River Adobe Inn

3151 West Main Street, Farmington, NM 87401 — *505-325-8219*
Diana Ohlson & David Beers, Resident Owners — *800-382-9251*
Some French, German, and Spanish spoken — *FAX 505-325-5074*

LOCATION	The inn is between Apache Street and LaPlata Highway (Highway 170), on the west side of Farmington.
OPEN	All year
DESCRIPTION	A 1985 adobe inn with massive wooden timbers, hand-built doors, wood ceilings, and southwestern furnishings, surrounded by River Side Park.
NO. OF ROOMS	Three rooms with private bathrooms.
RATES	Year-round rates for a single or double are $65-125, and the suite is $125. Cancellation requires two weeks' notice.
CREDIT CARDS	American Express, MasterCard, Visa
BREAKFAST	Continental plus is served in the dining room and includes fresh-ground gourmet coffees, English and Chinese teas, juice, fruit, and baked pastries.
AMENITIES	Air conditioning, small meeting facilities, afternoon or evening tea. The suite is handicapped accessible.
RESTRICTIONS	No smoking, children over 12 are welcome. The shepherd/Lab mix is Tewa and the Maine coon cat is Zappa.
REVIEWED	*The Complete Guide to Bed & Breakfasts, Inns & Guesthouses of the United States, Canada, and Worldwide*
MEMBER	Professional Association of Innkeepers International, Northwest New Mexico Bed & Breakfast Association

GALISTEO

(SANTA FE)

This tiny Spanish village hasn't changed all that much in the last couple of hundred years. Twenty-three miles south of Santa Fe on Highway 41, via Highway 285.

THE GALISTEO INN

9 La Vega Street, Galisteo, NM 87540 *505-466-4000*
Joanna & Wayne Aarniokoski, Resident Owners *FAX 505-466-4008*
Spanish spoken

LOCATION	From Santa Fe, take I-25 north to Highway 285, then drive south to Highway 41, and go south again to Galisteo. Once in town, take the first left, onto La Vega Street.
OPEN	All year except early January to early February
DESCRIPTION	A 1740 territorial adobe inn decorated with southwestern furnishings, located on 8 acres near Galisteo Creek.
NO. OF ROOMS	Nine rooms with private bathrooms and three rooms share two bathrooms. The Cottonwood Cottage is the best room in the house.
RATES	Year-round rates for a single or double with a private bathroom are $115-190, a single or double with a shared bathroom is $70-115, and the guesthouse is $190. There is a minimum stay on most weekends and cancellation requires 14 days' notice.
CREDIT CARDS	Discover, MasterCard, Visa
BREAKFAST	Full buffet breakfast is served in the dining room.
AMENITIES	Fifty-foot lap pool, outdoor hot tub, indoor sauna, robes, hammocks, mountain bikes, cookies, fruit, and beverages.
RESTRICTIONS	No pets, children over six are welcome. The golden retriever is called Chevy and the cat is called Rudy; there are also seven horses and two sheep.
REVIEWED	*America's Wonderful Little Hotels & Inns; Inns of the Southwest; Southern Living* magazine; *Country Living* magazine; *Country Inns*
MEMBER	New Mexico Bed & Breakfast Association, Professional Association of Innkeepers International
RATED	AAA 3 Diamonds, Mobil 3 Stars
KUDOS/COMMENTS	"Magical country inn 30 minutes from Santa Fe, riding, pool, first class." "Beautiful 200-plus-year-old adobe, quiet location at the edge of the village, towering cottonwood trees, excellent dinners." (1996)

HILLSBORO

About 30 miles southwest of Truth or Consequences via I-25 and Highway 152, this village offers the Spring Adventure in May, with arts and crafts, a parade, music, plays, and games; the Apple Festival on Labor Day weekend; and a lovely display of Christmas luminarios.

THE ENCHANTED VILLA INN BED & BREAKFAST

686 Main Street, Hillsboro, NM 88042 — *505-895-5686*
Maree Westland, Resident Owner — *FAX 505-895-5686*
EMAIL ebby@zianet.com

LOCATION — From I-25, take exit 63 and head west for 18 miles.

OPEN — All year

DESCRIPTION — A 1941 two-story territorial adobe with large, spacious, and well-lit common rooms and territorial furnishings.

NO. OF ROOMS — Three rooms with private bathrooms and two rooms share one bathroom. Try the Apache Room.

RATES — Year-round rates are $40 for a single and $70 for a double with a private or shared bathroom. The suite is $150. There is no minimum stay and cancellation requires seven days' notice.

CREDIT CARDS — No

BREAKFAST — Full breakfast is served in the dining room and includes soufflés, quiches, casseroles, burritos, biscuits, rolls, fresh fruit, and fresh-ground coffee.

AMENITIES — Facilities for meetings, reunions, weddings, and receptions; video library with over 500 movies; games; beverages; two secluded patios; generous front yard; handicapped accessible.

RESTRICTIONS — No smoking in guestrooms, no pets (kennel available on premises). Children of all ages are welcome. Crib, high chair, and toy box are available. The resident cat is called Cotton.

REVIEWED — *Fodor's New Mexico; Best Little B&Bs & Inns of New Mexico; American Historic Inns; America's Most Charming Towns and Villages; Country Inns & B&Bs of the Southwest; Off the Beaten Path—New Mexico*

Jemez Springs

Nestled inside the walls of the Jemez River canyon, this tiny resort town with mineral springs is surrounded by amazing natural sights. Don't miss Soda Dam, Jemez Cave, and Battleship Rock or the Jemez and Zia Pueblos. From Albuquerque, 62 miles north via I-25 and Highways 44 and 4.

The Dancing Bear Bed & Breakfast

314 San Diego Loop, Jemez Springs, NM 87025 — *505-829-3336*
WEBSITE www.virtualcities.com/nm/dancingbear.htm — *800-422-3271*

KUDOS/COMMENTS "Fabulous! Great! Wonderful! Warm, friendly! Fantastic environment." (1994) "Great place for quiet getaway, absolutely charming owner, Carol Breen." (1996) "Views to take your breath away. Comfortable surroundings, interesting artwork. Great food. It's where I go to relax." "Comfortable, real, unpretentious. A lovely experience." (1999)

Desert Willow Bed & Breakfast

15975 Scenic Highway #4, Jemez Springs, NM 87025 — *505-829-3410*
EMAIL wilsons@desertwillowbandb.com
WEBSITE www.desertwillowbandb.com

Elk Mountain Lodge Bed & Breakfast

37485 Highway 126, La Cueva, NM 87025 — *505-829-3159*
Terry Stright, Innkeeper — *800-815-2859*
Some Spanish spoken
EMAIL elkmountain@jemez.com
WEBSITE www.jemez.com/elkmountain

LOCATION Look for the sign at the intersection of Highways 4 and 126. The inn is 0.5 mile west, on Highway 126.

OPEN All year

DESCRIPTION Two log buildings, constructed in 1993 and 1998, with rustic, high-beamed ceilings, set amongst the tall ponderosa pines.

NO. OF ROOMS Five rooms with private bathrooms.

RATES	Summer rates for a single or double are $78-159. Winter rates (November through March) are less. Ask about a cancellation policy.
CREDIT CARDS	MasterCard, Visa
BREAKFAST	Continental breakfast is served in the lobby and includes hot and cold cereals, fruit, coffee, and more.
AMENITIES	Jacuzzi tubs in four bathrooms, candles, coffee-makers, wine glasses, radio, TV/VCR, phone upon request, backgammon, checkers, cards, and "personalized service."
RESTRICTIONS	None. "A romantic hideaway hardly needs children, but we'll do a roll-away for 'quiet' children if necessary."

RIVER DANCER INN

16445 Highway 4, Jemez Springs, NM 87025 — *505-829-3262*
Larry & Rose Ann Clutter, Resident Owners — *800-809-3262*
WEBSITE www.riverdancer.com — *FAX 505-829-3262*

LOCATION	Drive 11 miles north of Albuquerque on I-25, turn left on Highway 44, and go 22 miles to the town of San Ysidro. Turn right on Scenic Highway 4, and go north for 16 miles to the B&B on the left.
OPEN	All year
DESCRIPTION	A 1994 Native American–style inn on the Jemez River with a courtyard spring. Furnished with museum-quality Native American furnishings.
NO. OF ROOMS	Six rooms with private bathrooms.
RATES	Year-round rates for a single or double with a private bathroom are $69-89, a suite is $89-109, and a guesthouse is $79-159. There is no minimum stay and cancellation requires 14 days' notice, 30 days for holidays.
CREDIT CARDS	American Express, Carte Blanche, Diners Club, Discover, MasterCard, Visa
BREAKFAST	Full all-you-can-eat country breakfast is served in the dining room.
AMENITIES	Air conditioning, phone, TV/VCR, meeting facilities, gym, massage, hot tub, Jacuzzi, ceiling fans, candy and Indian "worry dolls" on every pillow, free 55-item refreshment bar, two rooms are handicapped accessible.
RESTRICTIONS	No smoking, no pets

MEMBER New Mexico Bed & Breakfast Association, Albuquerque Bed & Breakfast Association, Professional Association of Innkeepers International, American Bed & Breakfast Association, National Bed & Breakfast Association

RATED AAA 3 Diamonds

KINGSTON

Once the largest city in New Mexico Territory, Kingston's current population hovers around 25. Caballo Lake State Park is 30 miles east. About 50 miles southwest of Truth or Consequences, on scenic Highway 152, via I-25.

THE BLACK RANGE LODGE

---

119 Main Street, Kingston, NM 88042 *505-895-5652*
Catherine Wanek & Pete Fust, Resident Owners *FAX 505-895-3326*
Japanese and Spanish spoken
EMAIL *blackrange@zianet.com*

LOCATION Less than a half mile west of Highway 152 and Main Street, in the only three-story building in town.

OPEN All year

DESCRIPTION An 1884 three-story mountain lodge of brick and stone construction that offers a glimpse into a ghost town's past.

NO. OF ROOMS Seven rooms with private bathrooms and five rooms share four bathrooms. Catherine and Pete suggest room 2.

RATES Year-round rates are $60-80 for a single or double. Rates are subject to change. Please call for cancellation information.

CREDIT CARDS Discover, MasterCard, Visa

BREAKFAST Full breakfast is served in the dining room and features natural foods, including fresh-made breads and homemade jams and jellies. Catering is also available.

AMENITIES Separate guesthouse built using the straw-bale wall technique, green-chile popcorn and homemade ice cream on request, two large conference rooms and free Frisbee lesson from a Guiness Book record holder, free video games, pool table, and solar-heated hot tub.

RESTRICTIONS No smoking. Nimbus and Jazz are the American shorthair cats. There are 20 free-range chickens and 10 turkeys roaming the property.

REVIEWED	*Fodor's, Frommer's*
KUDOS/COMMENTS	"Historic old lodge. Funky, very casual, and fun, at the entrance to the beautiful Gila Wilderness." (1996)

LAS CRUCES

Just north of the Mexico–Texas border via I-25 or I-10, this agricultural center in the Mesilla Valley is the place to be for pecans and chilis. It is home to New Mexico State University, and charming Mesilla is only three miles west. Take in the Mesilla Valley Balloon Festival in January, the Wine and Chili War Festival in May, the Southern New Mexico State Fair in September, and the Whole Enchilada Fiesta and International Mariachi Convention and concert in October. Beautiful White Sands National Monument lies on the east side of San Augustin Pass on scenic Highway 70.

HAPPY TRAILS

1857 Paisano Road, Old Mesilla, NM 88005 *505-527-8471*
Sylvia Byrnes, Resident Owner
WEBSITE www.las-cruces-new-mexico.com

KUDOS/COMMENTS	"Newly remodeled adobe style with swimming pool on 10 acres of farm land." (1996)

HILLTOP HACIENDA BED & BREAKFAST

2600 Westmoreland Avenue, Las Cruces, NM 88012 *505-382-3556*
Teddi & Bob Peters, Innkeepers *FAX 505 382-3556*
Some Spanish spoken
EMAIL hilltop@zianet.com
WEBSITE www.travelassist.com/reg/nm102.html

LOCATION	From I-25, take exit 6A going east. Go north on Del Rey for exactly 3 miles. Del Rey turns into La Reina. At Westmoreland, turn right (east) and continue 1 mile.
OPEN	All year
DESCRIPTION	A 1966 two-story Spanish, red adobe lodge decorated with a mix of antiques and Southwest and original art, situated on 20 acres with spectacular views and garden paths.
NO. OF ROOMS	Three rooms with private bathrooms. Try the Southwest Room.

RATES	Year-round rates are $75-85 for a single or double and $210 for the guesthouse. There is no minimum stay and cancellation requires 14 days' notice.
CREDIT CARDS	American Express, Discover, MasterCard, Visa
BREAKFAST	Full breakfast is served in the dining room or on the garden deck and includes the house specialties: Teddi's Dutch babies, delicious green-chile quiche, omelets, and crepes, served with pastries, juice, coffee, and tea. Special diets are accommodated.
AMENITIES	Fully equipped guest kitchen, video and book libraries, cable TV in sitting room, free local calls, limited handicapped access, ceiling fans in each room, evening desserts when requested, beautiful walking trails (great for runners and hikers).
RESTRICTIONS	No smoking, no pets. Children are welcome when all three rooms are rented by one party. Willy is the resident poodle mix; Noelle and Nuggie are the cats. "The cats are outside cats and do not come inside the guest quarters. The dog stays inside the owners' area."
REVIEWED	*Gateway* magazine; *Frommer's New Mexico*
MEMBER	New Mexico Bed & Breakfast Association
RATED	AAA 3 Diamonds
KUDOS/COMMENTS	"Fantastic views of Organ Mountains." "Wonderful birds come to the feeder, great to be in the country yet close to town, good place for joggers to stay." "Caring hosts make you feel right at home, breathtaking views, especially at sunset and at night." (1996)

LODGE ON THE DESERT

215 South Weinrich Road, Las Cruces, NM 88005 — *505-523-9605*
LaVerne Tromble, Innkeeper — *FAX 505-541-1531*
EMAIL *laverne@lodge-on-the-desert*
WEBSITE *www.lodge-on-the-desert.com*

LOCATION	From I-10, take exit 135 to Highway 70. Go east, then go south on Weinrich, to the dead end.
OPEN	All year
DESCRIPTION	A 1961 three-story southwestern-style lodge with pink stucco and turquoise trim, brick and tile floors, antique furnishings throughout, fountains and gardens, and views of mountain ranges and twinkling city lights.
NO. OF ROOMS	Four rooms with private bathrooms.

RATES	Year-round rates are $55-95 for a single or double. There is no minimum stay and cancellation requires two days' notice.
BREAKFAST	Continental breakfast is served in the dining room and includes coffee, tea, juice, fresh fruit, breads, cereals, and milk.
AMENITIES	Robes, conference room, laundry and office facilities, outdoor kitchen with barbecue, large patio areas, pond, luxury linens, fully equipped workout facility.
RESTRICTIONS	No smoking, children over 15 are welcome. Belle, Joseph, and Dolly are the resident shepherd dogs.

Lundeen Inn of the Arts

618 South Alameda Boulevard, Las Cruces, NM 88005 *505-526-3326*
Linda & Gerald Lundeen, Innkeepers *888-526-3326 (reservations only)*
Spanish spoken *FAX 505-647-1334*
EMAIL *lundeen@innofthearts.com* WEBSITE *www.innofthearts.com*

LOCATION	From I-25, take the Lohman exit, turn right, go 2 miles, and turn left on Alameda.
OPEN	All year
DESCRIPTION	A 1910 two-story territorial hacienda with southwestern and antique furnishing and rooms named and decorated after southwestern artists.
NO. OF ROOMS	Twenty rooms with private bathrooms.
RATES	Year-round rates for a single or double are $58-85 and suites are $85-125. There is no minimum stay and cancellation requires 48 hours' notice.
CREDIT CARDS	American Express, Diners Club, Discover, MasterCard, Visa.
BREAKFAST	Full breakfast is served in the dining room and includes fruit, yogurt and almonds, muffins, bagels, and a daily special such as stuffed French toast, huevos rancheros, or pancakes.
AMENITIES	Afternoon refreshments, air conditioning, phones, most rooms have TVs, some rooms have fireplaces, art gallery, lecture rooms.
RESTRICTIONS	No smoking. Call about children and pets.
REVIEWED	*Bed & Breakfast Guide—Southwest: Arizona, New Mexico, Texas; New Mexico* magazine
RATED	AAA 3 Diamonds, Mobil 2 Stars
KUDOS/COMMENTS	"A well-run, interesting B&B. The owners are experienced." (1996)

MESON DE MESILLA

1803 Avenida de Mesilla, Mesilla, NM 88046 — *505-525-9212*
Raul Martinez, Innkeeper — *800-732-6025*
Spanish spoken — *FAX 505-527-4196*

LOCATION	Three-quarters-of-a-mile west of I-10 on the left side, heading into Old Mesilla.
OPEN	All year
DESCRIPTION	A 1985 two-story Spanish colonial guesthouse with elegant antiques and a second-floor balcony that offers breathtaking views of the Organ Mountains.
NO. OF ROOMS	Fifteen rooms with private bathrooms. Try the Kiva Room.
RATES	April through October, rates are $92 for a single or double and $140 for a suite. November through January, rates are $87 for a single or double and $135 for a suite. There is no minimum stay and cancellation requires 48 hours' notice.
CREDIT CARDS	American Express, Diners Club, Discover, MasterCard, Visa
BREAKFAST	Full gourmet breakfast is served in the dining room and includes a chef's choice of three entrées. Lunch and dinner are also available.
AMENITIES	Brass beds, ceiling fans, all rooms with telephones and cable TV.
RESTRICTIONS	No smoking, ask about pets
MEMBER	New Mexico Bed & Breakfast Association
RATED	AAA 3 Diamonds

T. R. H. SMITH MANSION BED & BREAKFAST

909 North Alameda Boulevard, Las Cruces, NM 88005 — *505-525-2525*
Jay & MarleneTebo, Resident Owners — *800-526-1914*
German spoken — *FAX 505-524-8227*
EMAIL smithmansion@zianet.com
WEBSITE www.smithmansion.com

LOCATION	From I-25, take the Main Street exit (US 70) and go to Picacho Avenue (also US 70), go 1 block to Alamada, turn right, and take an immediate left to the B&B.
OPEN	All year

T. R. H. Smith Mansion, Las Cruces

DESCRIPTION	A 1914 Mediterranean listed on both the State and National Historic Registers.
NO. OF ROOMS	Three rooms with private bathrooms.
RATES	Year-round rates for a single or double are $70-100. There is a midweek discount. There is no minimum stay and cancellation requires seven days' notice.
CREDIT CARDS	American Express, Discover, MasterCard, Visa
BREAKFAST	Full breakfast is served in the dining room and includes German-style homemade breads, lots of fruit, cheeses, smoked meats, and eggs, plus a baked entrée such as French toast, waffles, frittata, coffee, and tea.
AMENITIES	All rooms are air conditioned, oversized beds, turndown service, pool table in basement, in-room telephones with data ports.
RESTRICTIONS	No smoking, no pets, children over 10 are welcome. One pet and younger children are okay if no other rooms are occupied. The Keeshond mix is called Christie and she loves company.
MEMBER	Professional Association of Innkeepers International
KUDOS/COMMENTS	"Wonderful turn-of-the-century mansion with charming hosts."

Valley Vista Bed & Breakfast, Las Cruces

VALLEY VISTA BED & BREAKFAST

17430 Highway 70 East, Las Cruces, NM 88011 — *505-382-8103*
Art & Barbara Gutzman, Innkeepers — *800-797-0575*

LOCATION	From Las Cruces, go east on Highway 70 approximately 14 miles to milepost 163.3.
OPEN	All year
DESCRIPTION	A 1993 western ranch-style inn built with brick and stone, on a mountain slope on 2 desert-landscaped acres.
NO. OF ROOMS	Four rooms with private bathrooms.
RATES	Year-round rates are $72 for a single or double. There is no minimum stay and cancellation requires eight days' notice, 30 days during holidays.
CREDIT CARDS	American Express, Discover, MasterCard, Visa
BREAKFAST	All food and beverages for a full breakfast are provided, including juice, milk, coffee, tea, eggs, bacon, sausage, bread, and mixes for pancakes, waffles, muffins, and biscuits. Guests prepare their own breakfasts.
AMENITIES	Suites with private entrances, kitchens, living rooms, TV, phone, central air conditioning and heating, filtered water, views, patio with porch swings, large deck, front porch, wildlife viewing.
RESTRICTIONS	No smoking inside, no pets inside. Licorice is the resident black cat.

LAS VEGAS

Once the hangout of famous desperados, this Las Vegas is a beautiful, restored Victorian town boasting more than 900 buildings on the National Historic Register and five historic districts. Check out Rails and Trails in June, the People's Fair in August, the Places with a Past historic building tour in August, and the Wildflower Festival in September. Visit the Las Vegas National Wildlife Refuge, well known for its raptors, and take a dip in Montezuma Hot Springs. Las Vegas is an hour east of Santa Fe, on I-25.

CARRIAGE HOUSE

925 Sixth Street, Las Vegas, NM 87701 — *505-454-1784*
Anne & John Bradford, Resident Owners

LOCATION	Less than a half mile from the University exit, 1 block from Carnegie Library Park.
OPEN	All year
DESCRIPTION	A restored 1893 three-story Queen Anne Victorian with Victorian furnishings.
NO. OF ROOMS	Three rooms with private bathrooms and two rooms share one bathroom. Anne recommends the Pink Room.
RATES	Year-round rates for a single or double with a private bathroom are $69-79, and rates for a single or double with a shared bathroom are $59-69. There is no minimum stay and cancellation requires seven days' notice.
CREDIT CARDS	American Express, Discover, MasterCard, Visa
BREAKFAST	Continental plus is served in the dining room and includes home-baked breads, muffins, homemade granola, fresh fruit, and coffeecakes.
AMENITIES	Robes provided for shared bathrooms.
RESTRICTIONS	Smoking on the porch only, no pets
REVIEWED	*New Mexico Handbook; Recommended Country Inns—The Southwest; Off the Beaten Path—New Mexico*

PLAZA HOTEL

230 Old Town Plaza, Las Vegas, NM 87701 — *505-425-3591*
Wid & Katherine Slick, Owners — *FAX 505-425-9659*
EMAIL plazahotel@worldplaces.com

LINCOLN

Sixty miles west of Roswell on scenic Highway 380, this town is the site of the Billy the Kid Pageant during the first weekend in August, the Golden Aspen Rally for motorcycles in September, the Hubbard Museum of the American West, and the Lincoln Heritage Museum.

CASA DE PATRON B&B INN

Highway 380 East, Lincoln, NM 88338 — *505-653-4676*
Jerry & Cleis Jordan, Innkeepers — *800-524-5202*
EMAIL patron@pvtnetworks.net — *FAX 505-653-4671*
WEBSITE www.casapatron.com

LOCATION	In the village of Lincoln, on the south side of Highway 380.
OPEN	All year
DESCRIPTION	An 1860 contemporary territorial adobe inn with two casitas, decorated with southwestern furnishings, antiques, and collectibles; surrounded by courtyards on 5 acres of gardens.
NO. OF ROOMS	Seven rooms with private bathrooms.
RATES	Year-round rates for a single or double are $74-117. The two casitas rent for $97-107 for a double. There is a minimum stay on some major holidays. Ask about a cancellation policy.
CREDIT CARDS	MasterCard, Visa
BREAKFAST	Full breakfast is served in the dining room for guests of the B&B. Continental plus is served for guests of the casitas. Lunch, dinner, and special meals are available by special arrangements.
AMENITIES	Upon arrival, hot apple cider (winter) or cold lemonade (summer), fresh flowers, homemade candy or cookies, handmade soap, bubble bath in rooms with tubs, hiking trail, conference room, one room handicapped accessible, double Jacuzzi in one room and fireplace in two rooms.
RESTRICTIONS	No smoking, no pets. The cat is called Fluff and the collie/chow mix is called Teddie.
REVIEWED	*America's Wonderful Little Hotels & Inns; Recommended Country Inns—The Southwest; Frommer's New Mexico; Fodor's The Southwest; Off the Beaten Path—New Mexico; Recommended Romantic Inns*
MEMBER	New Mexico Bed & Breakfast Association, Professional Association of Innkeepers International

RATED AAA 3 Diamonds, Mobil 3 Stars

KUDOS/COMMENTS "One of the oldest (perhaps the oldest) B&B in Lincoln County. Very much the image of a Southwest casita-style inn, lovely setting." "Warm, welcoming innkeepers, attractive rooms." "Great hosts, a warm feeling as you walk in, a great location." (1996)

THE ELLIS STORECOUNTRY INN

Milepost 98, Highway 380, Lincoln, NM 88338 — *505-653-4609*
David Vigil, Innkeeper — *800-653-6460*
Spanish spoken — *FAX 505-653-4610*
EMAIL ellistore@pvtnetworks.net — *WEBSITE www.ellisstore.com*

LOCATION Located at the east end of Lincoln, 35 miles north of Ruidoso.

OPEN All year

DESCRIPTION An 1850 Lincoln territorial inn made up of three buildings with Southwest Victorian decor. Listed on the National and State Historic Registers.

NO. OF ROOMS Six rooms with private bathrooms and four rooms share two bathrooms. Try the Dr. James Room.

RATES Year-round rates are $109-139 for a single or double with a private bathroom, $79-89 for a single or double with a shared bathroom, and $119-130 for a suite. There is a minimum stay during holidays and special events. Cancellation requires seven days' notice.

CREDIT CARDS American Express, Discover, MasterCard, Visa

BREAKFAST Full gourmet breakfast is cooked to order and served in the dining room. Gourmet meals are available by reservation, Wednesday through Saturday.

RESTRICTIONS No smoking, no pets, children over 12 are welcome. Spook, Colonel Fritz, and Guy are the resident cats.

KUDOS/COMMENTS "A gracious veranda and garden with a sprawling lawn. Ginny is a superb cook and offers big, leisurely, sumptuous dinners." (1996)

Los Alamos

Thirty-five miles northwest of Santa Fe via Highways 285 and 502, this is the home of Los Alamos National Laboratories, where a group of very smart people gathered during World War II to build weapons of mass destruction. Check out the Bradbury Science Museum, the Fuller Lodge Art Center, and the Los Alamos County Historical Museum. Bandelier National Monument and Puye Indian Ruins are close by, and Pajarito ski area boasts 21 challenging runs.

Adobe Pines Bed & Breakfast

2101 Loma Linda Drive, Los Alamos, NM 87544 — *505-662-6761*
Dan Partin, Innkeeper — *FAX 603-754-2484*
EMAIL AdobePines@LosAlamos.com
WEBSITE www.losalamos.com/adobepines

LOCATION	Ten minutes from Los Alamos National Laboratory.
OPEN	All year
DESCRIPTION	A 1992 two-story adobe pueblo host home with comfortable, elegant furnishings.
NO. OF ROOMS	Three rooms with private bathrooms and two rooms share a bathroom.
RATES	Year-round rates are $71-78 for a single or double with a private or shared bathroom. There is no minimum stay and cancellation requires 24 hours' notice.
CREDIT CARDS	American Express, Discover, MasterCard, Visa
BREAKFAST	Continental plus is served in the dining room and includes coffee, juice, fruit, microwave hotcakes and waffles, bagels, hot and cold cereals, and English muffins.
RESTRICTIONS	No smoking, no pets, no children

Bud's Bed & Breakfast

1981 C North Road, Los Alamos, NM 87544 — *505-662-4239*
James Farley, Resident Owner — *800-581-2837*
Functional French and Spanish spoken
EMAIL budsbb@aol.com
WEBSITE www.vla.com/buds

LOCATION	When coming into Los Alamos from the east, stay on Trinity Drive until you reach Diamond Drive. Turn right onto Diamond and

continue about 0.5 mile until you reach Urban Street. Turn left and go up three blocks to North Road. Turn left onto North Road and park at the tennis courts.

OPEN	All year
DESCRIPTION	A two-story shingled fourplex with abundant gardens and a year-round greenhouse.
NO. OF ROOMS	Two rooms with private bathrooms and four rooms share two bathrooms.
RATES	Year-round rates are $65-75 for a single or double with a private bathroom and $55-65 for a single or double with a shared bathroom. A suite is $80. There is no minimum stay and cancellation requires 48 hours' notice.
CREDIT CARDS	American Express, MasterCard, Visa
BREAKFAST	Full breakfast is served in the dining room and is prepared by James, a professional cook for 35 years. Breakfasts are homemade and served to order.
AMENITIES	Hot tub, sauna, access to all the produce from the gardens, fresh flowers in season, access to outdoor pool, bicycles, tennis, air conditioning.
RESTRICTIONS	No smoking, no pets

CANYON INN BED & BREAKFAST

80 Canyon Road, Los Alamos, NM 87544 — *505-662-9595*
Rich Kraemer, Resident Owner — *800-662-2565*

LOCATION	Take Highway 4 into town, go 0.5 mile beyond the Los Alamos Airport sign and turn right at a fork. The inn is the third house on the right, across from the park.
OPEN	All year
DESCRIPTION	A 1958 ranch house located in a residential area near town.
NO. OF ROOMS	Four rooms with private bathrooms.
RATES	Year-round rate for a single or double is $55. There is no minimum stay and cancellation requires seven days' notice.
CREDIT CARDS	American Express, MasterCard, Visa
BREAKFAST	Continental plus is self-serve and available anytime.
AMENITIES	Kitchen where guests may prepare their own meals, laundry facilities, and deck.
RESTRICTIONS	No smoking, no pets, children over seven are welcome.

Casa del Rey

305 Rover Boulevard, Los Alamos, NM 87544 — *505-672-9401*
Virginia King, Resident Owner
EMAIL *vlking@aol.com*

LOCATION	From Highway 502, take the White Rock/Bandelier exit and go 4 miles, turning left at Rover Boulevard. Drive 1 mile, to the corner of Rover and Kendall.
OPEN	All year
DESCRIPTION	A 1971 southwestern adobe-style host home with contemporary furnishings and a garden courtyard.
NO. OF ROOMS	Two rooms share one bathroom.
RATES	Year-round rates are $35 for a single and $45 for a double. There is no minimum stay and cancellation requires four days' notice.
CREDIT CARDS	No
BREAKFAST	Continental plus is served on the sun porch or patios and includes juice, fruit, homemade granola and breads, cereals, coffee, tea, or other hot drinks.
AMENITIES	Beautiful flower gardens, patios for watching birds or viewing mountains, clear night skies for stargazing, cold or hot drinks, and cookies.
RESTRICTIONS	No smoking, no pets, children over five are welcome. Chester is the resident orange tabby.
REVIEWED	*Bed & Breakfast USA; The Complete Guide to Bed & Breakfasts, Inns & Guesthouses in the United States, Canada, and Worldwide*

Castillo del Alba, A Bed & Breakfast Near Bandelier

135 La Senda Road, Los Alamos, NM 87544 — *505-672-9494*
Anna Earlene & Roland Caspersen, Innkeepers — *FAX 505-672-2085*
EMAIL *caspersen@earthlink.net* — WEBSITE *www.bandelierbandb.com*

LOCATION	About 30 minutes from Santa Fe.
OPEN	All year
DESCRIPTION	A two-story Mediterranean guesthome with a red-tile roof and a tower entry with European decor, overlooking the Rio Grande gorge.

NO. OF ROOMS	Four rooms with private bathrooms.
RATES	Please ask about current rates and cancellation information. There is a two-night minimum stay.
CREDIT CARDS	MasterCard, Visa
BREAKFAST	Full gourmet breakfast is served in the formal dining room.
AMENITIES	Outside private entrances, 2 acres with hiking down to the Rio Grande, grand piano, extensive library, bicycles, bird-watching and stargazing, gardens, tremendous views.
RESTRICTIONS	No smoking, no pets. Guests with pets can be referred to a local veterinarian who will board pets.

North Road Bed & Breakfast

2127 North Road, Los Alamos, NM 87544 — *505-662-3678*
Katherine Mockler, Resident Owner

Patio Garden

4756 Trinity Drive, Los Alamos, NM 87544 — *505-662-9581*

Renata's Orange Street Bed & Breakfast

3496 Orange Street, Los Alamos, NM 87544 — *505-662-2651*
Lynda Hartman, Innkeeper — *800-662-3180*
EMAIL *renatas@losalamos.com* — *FAX 505-661-1538*
WEBSITE *www.losalamos.com/orangestreetinn*

LOCATION	Highway 502 becomes Trinity Drive. Take Trinity to Diamond Drive and turn right onto Diamond. At the second stoplight, turn right onto Orange Street. Go downhill about a block to the first residence on the left, a blue house with white picket fence.
OPEN	All year
DESCRIPTION	A 1950 two-story government inn with Southwest and country decor, located on a finger mesa with forest views and a 150-foot-deep canyon behind the B&B.

NO. OF ROOMS Five rooms with private bathrooms and four rooms share two bathrooms. Try La Casita Room.

RATES Year-round rates are $65-69 for a single or double with a private bathroom, $50-55 for a single or double with a shared bathroom, and $75-99 for a suite. There is no minimum stay and cancellation requires 72 hours' notice.

CREDIT CARDS American Express, Diners Club, Discover, MasterCard, Visa

BREAKFAST Full breakfast is served in the dining room and includes coffeecake and bread, yogurt, fresh fruit, cold cereals, and a hot entrée such as quiche or crepes, plus coffee, tea, and juice.

AMENITIES Evening wine and hors d'oeuvres featuring freshly made salsa, hiking guide for exploring trails that begin at the door, luxurious Turtlewear robes, down comforters, bikes, can arrange for massage, discounts at local Olympic-size pool and YMCA.

RESTRICTIONS No smoking, children over two are welcome. Pets may be allowed in private entrance suite.

MADRID

About 30 minutes south of Santa Fe on Highway 14, Madrid was a coal company town famous for its Christmas lights and decorations, which were powered by more than 500,000 kilowatt hours of coal-generated electricity. In 1975, the coal company sold the town, which is now inhabited by artists and craftspeople. The town is still famous for its Christmas Festival of Lights. Check out the New Mexico Jazz and Blues Festival in August.

JAVA JUNCTION B&B

2855 Highway 14, Madrid, NM 87010 *505-438-2772*
Linda Dunnill, Innkeeper
WEBSITE www.java-junction.com

LOCATION On the historic Turquoise Trail, Highway 14, halfway between Albuquerque and Santa Fe, on Main Street above the Java Junction Coffee and Gift Shop.

OPEN All year

DESCRIPTION A 1915 two-story wood-frame Victorian apartment on the second floor of a beautifully restored old mining home, with a coffee and gift shop downstairs.

NO. OF ROOMS One full apartment with a private bathroom.

Java Junction B&B, Madrid

RATES	Year-round rates for a single or double are $55-65. There is no minimum stay. Ask about a cancellation fee.
CREDIT CARDS	MasterCard, Visa
BREAKFAST	Continental breakfast is served downstairs in the coffee shop and includes latte, cappuccino, other coffee drinks, refills, fresh homemade pastries, bagels, and muffins.
AMENITIES	Six-foot clawfoot tub, large private porch, full kitchen, microwave.
RESTRICTIONS	No smoking inside. Suzie and Holly are the resident shelties.

MADRID LODGING

14 Opera House Road, Madrid, NM 87010 *505-471-3450*
Joni & Greg Neutra, Resident Owners

NAGEEZI

A trading post, post office, and a B&B, at the gateway to Chaco Canyon. What more do you need? South of Aztec and the Colorado border, on scenic Highway 44.

CHACO INN AT THE POST

Highway 44 & County Road #7800, Nageezi, NM 87037 *505-632-3646*

DESCRIPTION	A 1939 large stone house with native southwestern furnishings.
NO. OF ROOMS	Two rooms with private bathrooms and four rooms share two bathrooms.
RATES	Please inquire about current rates and cancellation information.
CREDIT CARDS	MasterCard, Visa
BREAKFAST	Full breakfast served.
AMENITIES	Hammocks, walking and biking trails.
RESTRICTIONS	No smoking
KUDOS/COMMENTS	"Entrance to Chaco Canyon. The inn is very basic but the food is excellent." (1996)

NOGAL

MONJEAU SHADOWS COUNTRY INN

HC 67, Box 87, Nogal, NM 88341 *505-336-4191*
Billie Reidland, Manager

KUDOS/COMMENTS "Lovely house, gracious hosts, quiet, view." (1996)

Ojo Caliente

Five different mineral hot springs and numerous swimming pools, plus the Anasazi Indian Ruins are all excellent reasons to stay here, 24 miles north of Española on Highway 285.

The Inn & Mercantile at Ojo

Hot Springs Road, Ojo Caliente, NM 87549 — *505-583-9131*
Claudia Page, Innkeeper
Spanish spoken
EMAIL innojo@ojocaliente.com
WEBSITE www.ojocaliente.com

LOCATION	Fifty-five miles north of Santa Fe on US Highway 285, turn west on Highway 414 toward Ojo Caliente Hot Springs and go 200 yards to the inn, across from the old adobe Catholic Church.
OPEN	All year
DESCRIPTION	A renovated 1950s-era northern New Mexico tin roof territorial furnished with iron beds and primitive pine wardrobes. Each room has an outside door to the courtyard.
NO. OF ROOMS	Six rooms with private bathrooms.
RATES	Year-round rates for a single or double are $65-85. There is a two-night minimum stay during weekends and cancellation requires 14 days' notice.
CREDIT CARDS	MasterCard, Visa
BREAKFAST	Full breakfast is served in the dining room and includes fresh-ground coffee, tea, fruit juices, fresh fruit in season, homemade breads and muffins or pancakes with maple syrup, breakfast meats, homemade granola, and yogurt. Special meals can be arranged for groups of six to eight people.
AMENITIES	Outdoor patio with fountain, Ping-Pong room, meeting room, breakfast visits from local historian, down comforters in most rooms.
RESTRICTIONS	No smoking, no pets, children over 12 are welcome.

PLACITAS

A small community on the north edge of the Sandia Crest, 20 miles northeast of Albuquerque via I-25 and Highway 165, and just east of Bernalillo.

HACIENDA DE PLACITAS B&B

491 Highway 165, Placitas, NM 87043 — *505-867-0082*
Carol Dinsmore Orfeo & Francois Orfeo, Resident Owners — *FAX 505-867-3775*
French spoken

LOCATION	From I-25, take exit 242 and go east on Highway 165 for 4.9 miles. Look for the landmark windmill and covered wagon at the entrance on the left.
OPEN	All year
DESCRIPTION	An adobe hacienda, over 100 years old, with private garden suites, an adobe casita, and vintage cowboy cabin. Decorated with Spanish and European furnishings.
NO. OF ROOMS	Five rooms with private bathrooms (three suites and two guesthouses).
RATES	Please inquire about current rates and cancellation information.
CREDIT CARDS	MasterCard, Visa
BREAKFAST	Full breakfast is served in the dining room.
AMENITIES	Hot tub, exercise room, mountainside pool, gardens, movie-set teepees, barbecue grills, trails, corporate facilities, wedding facilities, afternoon cocktails, private entrances, fireplaces, air conditioning, cable TV/VCR, coffee-makers, refrigerators, microwaves, robes, guesthouses have complete kitchens.
RESTRICTIONS	Smoking outdoors only, pets and children welcome.
REVIEWED	*Country Homes* magazine, *Best Places to Stay in the Southwest*
MEMBER	Professional Association of Innkeepers International, New Mexico Bed & Breakfast Association, Albuquerque Bed & Breakfast Association
RATED	AAA 3 Diamonds, Mobil 3 Stars
KUDOS/COMMENTS	"Gorgeous inn decorated by two artists with excellent taste in cooking and decorating." "This place is a dream world, a compound featuring southwestern antique decor in every detail." "Beautiful adobe main building, historic log cabin, gorgeous sunset views." (1996)

PORTALES

THE MORNING STAR INN

620 West 2nd Street, Portales, NM 88130 — *505-356-2994*
Dave & Tonya Williams, Resident Owners
EMAIL *morningstarbnb@yucca.net*
WEBSITE *www.pdrpip.com/morningstarb&b/index.htm*

RED RIVER

A year-round resort town nestled in the Carson National Forest, 35 miles northeast of Taos via Highways 52 and 38.

EL WESTERN LODGE

PO Box 301, Red River, NM 87558 — *505-754-2272*

LAZY MINER LODGE

PO Box 836, Red River, NM 87558 — *505-754-6444*
WEBSITE *home.att.net/~lazyminer* — *800-766-4637*

TELEMARK BED & BREAKFAST

609 River Street, Red River, NM 87558 — *505-754-2534*
Martha & Sigi Klein, Resident Owners — *FAX 505-754-2534*
German and Spanish spoken
WEBSITE *www.redrivernm.com/telemark*

LOCATION	One block off Main Street, at Caribel Trail and River Street.
OPEN	All year
DESCRIPTION	A 1991 two-story alpine lodge with alpine and southwestern decor, and balconies overlooking the river and ski slopes.

NO. OF ROOMS	Six rooms with private bathrooms.
RATES	November through March, rates are $90-120 for a single or double. Summer rates from April through October are $80-100 for a single or double. There is a minimum stay on holidays and cancellation requires 14 days' notice.
CREDIT CARDS	MasterCard, Visa
BREAKFAST	Full breakfast is served buffet style in the dining room and includes one main dish plus muffins, breads, and breakfast cakes.
AMENITIES	Hot tub next to the river, chaise lounges, outdoor fireplaces, large deck, hors d'oeuvres, tea in the afternoon, very close to ski slopes.
RESTRICTIONS	No smoking, no pets, children over 12 are welcome.

Regina

Regina Inn

906 Highway 96, Regina, NM 87046 *505-289-9195*

Rinconada

Forty-five miles north of Santa Fe, between Española and Taos on scenic Highway 68, Rinconada sits along the eastern bank of the Rio Grande beneath tall mesas and high, wind-shorn cliffs. This tiny town is wide spot along the road, consisting of little more than a fruit stand, a fire station, and a few adobe buildings.

Casa Rinconada Private Guest Houses

Box 10 A Taos Highway 68, Rinconada, NM 90731 *505-579-4466*
JoAnne de la Fuente, Innkeeper

LOCATION	In northern New Mexico, 20 miles south of Taos and 45 miles north of Santa Fe.
OPEN	All year
DESCRIPTION	A Southwest-style adobe guesthouse nestled in a mountain valley on the Rio Grande.

NO. OF ROOMS	All rooms with private bathrooms.
RATES	Rates are year-round. There is a two-night minimum stay. Ask about a cancellation policy.
CREDIT CARDS	No
BREAKFAST	Continental breakfast is provided in the private kitchen.

ROCIADA

TOTEM RANCH BED & BREAKFAST

Highway 105, Rociada, NM 87742 *505-425-8929*

SANDIA PARK
(ALBUQUERQUE)

The higher elevations of the Sandia Mountains make this a wonderful escape from greater downtown Albuquerque. Close to the Sandia Crest Ski Area and the Turquoise Trail.

ANGELS' ASCENT

20 Gilbert Place, Sandia Park, NM 87047 *505-286-1588*
Some Spanish spoken
WEBSITE www.showemall.com/showemall/angels

LOCATION	Three-and-a-half miles east of the entrance to the Sandia Crest Highway off Highway 14. Follow Frost Road and turn left on Camino Alto in the Sandia Knolls subdivision.
OPEN	All year
DESCRIPTION	A 1988 two-story mountain chalet with English country furnishings, two decks, and views.
NO. OF ROOMS	Three rooms share two bathrooms.
RATES	Rates for a single or double are $65-150. There is a two-night minimum stay on major holidays, and cancellation requires 14 days' notice.
CREDIT CARDS	No

BREAKFAST	Full breakfast is served in the dining room or on the deck and may include egg dishes, potatoes, pancakes or waffles, fruit, home-baked breads with homemade preserves and syrups. Lunch, dinner, and special meals are available.
AMENITIES	Flowers, mints, stationery, video library, nostalgic music library, extensive book collection, outdoor hot tub with 180-degree mountain view, deck overlooking waterfall, afternoon refreshments.
RESTRICTIONS	No smoking indoors, no pets indoors, children are welcome.

Turquoise Trail Bed & Breakfast

65 Harms Road, Sandia Park, NM 87047 — *505-281-3795*

Santa Fe

The nation's oldest capital city, 60 miles north of Albuquerque via I-25, Santa Fe is not the undiscovered treasure it once was, but it remains a treasure nonetheless, just slightly ransacked. Local and nearby events and places of interest include the Indian and Spanish Markets and pueblos, archaeological ruins, the Georgia O'Keefe and Folk Art Museums, and Bandelier and Pecos National Monuments. The local fiesta during the first week of September features the burning of Zozobra (Old Man Gloom). Hit the slopes at Santa Fe Ski Basin.

Adobe Abode

202 Chapelle, Santa Fe, NM 87501 — *505-983-3133*
Pat Harbour, Resident Owner — *FAX 505-986-0972*
Spanish spoken
EMAIL *adobebnb@sprynet.com*
WEBSITE *www.adobeabode.com*

LOCATION	From the St. Francis exit on I-25, go north 3 miles, turn right onto Cerrillos Road, and drive 3 blocks to Guadalupe. Turn left, go through the intersection at Alameda, go 2 more blocks to Johnson Street, turn right, then left onto Chapelle.
OPEN	All year
DESCRIPTION	A restored 1907 pueblo-style adobe with sophisticated southwestern decor and eclectic furnishings, located in a quiet residential neighborhood just four blocks from the Plaza.

NO. OF ROOMS	Six rooms with private bathrooms. Pat suggests the Cactus or Bronco Rooms.
RATES	Year-round rates are $110-160 for a single or double and $150-160 for a suite. There is a two-night minimum stay on weekends and cancellation requires 10 days' notice.
CREDIT CARDS	Discover, MasterCard, Visa
BREAKFAST	Full gourmet breakfast is served in the dining room and includes fresh-brewed coffee or a selection of teas, orange juice, fresh fruit, homemade muffins, and a hot entrée that changes daily.
AMENITIES	Designer bed linens, fluffy robes, private phones and cable TVs, some rooms with fireplaces and private patios, fax, free off-street parking, coffee- and tea-makers, complimentary sherry and Santa Fe cookies, good reading lights.
RESTRICTIONS	No smoking except outside, no pets.
REVIEWED	*Access Santa Fe, Taos & Albuquerque; America's Wonderful Little Hotels & Inns; Best Places to Stay in the Southwest; Fodor's Bed & Breakfasts and Country Inns—The Southwest; Frommer's Santa Fe, Taos, & Albuquerque; The Insider's Guide to Santa Fe; Journey to the High Southwest; Recommended Country Inns—The Southwest; The Santa Fe & Taos Book: A Complete Guide*
MEMBER	Santa Fe Inns of Distinction
RATED	AAA 3 Diamonds, Mobil 2 Stars

Adobe Retreat Bed & Breakfast

16 Amado Sueno, Sante Fe, NM 87505 — *505-474-7725*
Jim & Karla Blaine, Innkeepers — *FAX 505-474-3794*
EMAIL *jk.blaine@cwix.com*

LOCATION	Take exit 275 off of I-25 south and fork to the right. At the flashing yellow light, turn left, following the signs to the museum for 0.25 mile, and turn right onto Los Pinos Road. Drive 2.25 miles and turn left onto Amado Sueno.
OPEN	All year
DESCRIPTION	A 1997 pueblo-style adobe country inn with rooms that open up onto a quiet courtyard with views of the hills beyond.
NO. OF ROOMS	Three rooms with private bathrooms.
RATES	Year-round rates are $87-115 for a single or double. There is no minimum stay and cancellation requires seven days' notice.
CREDIT CARDS	Discover, MasterCard, Visa

BREAKFAST	Full breakfast is cooked to order and served in the dining room. Guests choose between omelets, pancakes, and Southwest specialties, plus fresh fruit and bakery goods. Special dietary needs can be accommodated with advance notice.
AMENITIES	Fresh flowers, candy, snacks (including fresh-baked brownies), soft drinks, teas, and juices in rooms; afternoon happy hour with wine or home-brewed beer; Great Room can accommodate meetings or receptions; handicapped accessible; fireplace in Great Room.
RESTRICTIONS	No smoking, no pets. G.G. and Herb are the resident cats and Boomer is the pointer.
MEMBER	New Mexico Bed & Breakfast Association

Alexander's Inn Bed & Breakfast

529 East Palace Avenue, Santa Fe, NM 87501 — *505-986-1431*
Carolyn Lee, Innkeeper — *888-321-5123*
French spoken — *FAX 505-982-8572*
EMAIL AlexandInn@aol.com
WEBSITE www.collectorsguide.com/alexandinn

LOCATION	From Albuquerque, take I-25 north and exit at St. Francis Drive. Follow St. Francis into town and turn right at Cerrillos Road. Turn right at Paseo de Peralta and follow it as it curves around to Palace Avenue. Turn right onto Palace Avenue. The inn is 3 blocks up and on the left.
OPEN	All year
DESCRIPTION	A 1903 two-story Craftsman inn with country cottage decor, including antiques, lace, and stenciling. The inn is surrounded by beautiful gardens of roses and lilacs.
NO. OF ROOMS	Eight rooms with private bathrooms and two rooms share one bathroom. Try the Lilac Room.
RATES	March 15 through November 14, rates are $125-150 for a single or double with a private bathroom, $90 for a single or double with a shared bathroom, and $150-165 for a suite. November 15 through March 14, rates are $100-135 for a single or double with a private bathroom, $75 for a single or double with a shared bathroom, and $135-150 for a suite. There is a two-night minimum stay on weekends, three nights during major holidays. Cancellation requires two weeks' notice, one month over major holidays.
CREDIT CARDS	Discover, MasterCard, Visa
BREAKFAST	Continental plus is served in the dining room and includes homemade granola, home-baked goodies, whole-grain breads, fresh fruit salad, yogurt, cheeses, and gourmet coffees.

AMENITIES	Soft robes, garden hot tub, nighttime chocolates, homemade cookies and goodies, near the Plaza, cable TV, phones, down comforters, fireplaces, concierge services, lovely gardens.
RESTRICTIONS	Children of all ages welcome in the back suites, children over five are welcome in the main house. Well-behaved pets are also welcome. Dolly is the resident Lab.
REVIEWED	*Fodor's, Frommer's, The Insider's Guide to Santa Fe*
MEMBER	New Mexico Bed & Breakfast Association, Santa Fe Inns of Distinction, Professional Association of Innkeepers International
RATED	AAA 3 Diamonds, Mobil 3 Stars
KUDOS/COMMENTS	"Warm hospitality in a Victorian setting." (1996) "A small, intimate adobe retreat just off the historic plaza."

Camas de Santa Fe

323 East Palace Avenue, Santa Fe, NM 87501 — *505-984-1337*
John Gundzik, Resident Owner — *800-632-2627*
EMAIL camas@travelbase.com — *505-984-8449*

NO. OF ROOMS	Fourteen rooms with private bathrooms; one room has a private bathroom across the hall.
RATES	Please inquire about current rates and cancellation information.
CREDIT CARDS	American Express, Discover, MasterCard, Visa
BREAKFAST	Expanded continental breakfast is served in the dining room.
RESTRICTIONS	No smoking

Casa de la Cuma Bed & Breakfast

105 Paseo de la Cuma, Santa Fe, NM 87501 — *888-366-1717*
Donna Hufton, Innkeeper — *FAX 505-983-2241*
Spanish spoken
EMAIL casacuma@swcp.com
WEBSITE www.casacuma.com/bb

LOCATION	Four blocks north of the Plaza.
OPEN	All year
DESCRIPTION	A 1950s adobe with patios, fireplaces, and views, furnished in the southwestern style.

NO. OF ROOMS	Two rooms with private bathrooms and two rooms share one bathroom.
RATES	June through October, rates are $125 for a single or double with a private bathroom, $85 for a single or double with a shared bathroom, and the suite is $135. November through May, rates are $105 for a single or double with a private bathroom, $75 for a single or double with a shared bathroom, and the suite is $115. There is a minimum stay on weekends during high season and cancellation requires 10 days' notice.
CREDIT CARDS	MasterCard, Visa
BREAKFAST	Continental plus is served in the dining room or guestrooms.
AMENITIES	Afternoon snacks on patios.
RESTRICTIONS	No smoking, children are welcome in the suite.
MEMBER	New Mexico Bed & Breakfast Association

Casa del Toro Bed & Breakfast

229 McKenzie Street, Sante Fe, NM 87501 *505-995-9689*
WEBSITE *www.casadeltoro.com/* *888-995-9689*
FAX 505-982-4475

Casa de Moya

332 Camino Cerrito, Santa Fe, NM 87501 *505-983-1023*
WEBSITE *www.sfol.com/sfol/realestate/vacation/moya.html* *800-767-3201*

Castillo Inn

622 Castillo Place, Santa Fe, NM 87501 *505-982-1212*
Kendra Weeks, Resident Owner
WEBSITE *www.trail.com/~castillo*

THE CHAPELLE STREET CASITAS

209 Chapelle Street, Santa Fe, NM 87501 — *505-988-2883*
Bruce Kuehnle, Innkeeper — *888-340-2883*
EMAIL *chapellecasitas@yahoo.com* — *FAX 505-988-2883*
WEBSITE *www.casitas.net*

LOCATION	From I-25, take the St. Francis north exit. Proceed north 4 miles to Alameda Street. Turn right (toward the mountains), drive 1 mile to Guadalupe, 0.5 mile to Johnson, and 0.1 mile to Chapelle. Turn left on Chapelle and go 2 blocks.
OPEN	All year
DESCRIPTION	Turn-of-the-century adobe bungalows built to house officers from Fort Marcy, with original wood floors and southwestern furniture and accents. Listed on the National and State Historic Registers.
NO. OF ROOMS	Four rooms with private bathrooms. Try Suite D.
RATES	May through October, rates are $125-145 for a single or double. November through April, rates are $95-115 for a single or double. There is a minimum stay and cancellation requires 14 days' notice.
CREDIT CARDS	Discover, MasterCard, Visa
BREAKFAST	Continental breakfast is served in the guestrooms and includes fruit plates, baked goods, cereal, milk, coffee, and juice.
AMENITIES	Air conditioning, robes, and "location, location, location—which means you do not have to hassle with plaza traffic and parking."
RESTRICTIONS	No smoking

CRYSTAL MESA FARM BED & BREAKFAST

3547 Highway 14, Santa Fe, NM 87505 — *505-474-5224*

DANCING GROUND OF THE SUN

711 Paseo de Peralto, Santa Fe, NM 87501 — *505-986-9797*
WEBSITE *www.dancingground.com* — *800-645-5673*

Delmar en la Cienega

50 Entrada la Cienega, Santa Fe, NM 87505 *505-471-6498*
EMAIL *delmarsf@webtv.net* WEBSITE *www.viconet.com/~tbonds/*

Don Gaspar Compound Inn

623 Don Gaspar, Santa Fe, NM 87501 *505-986-8664*
Shirley & David Alford, Innkeepers *888-986-8664*
Spanish and German spoken *FAX 505-986-0696*
EMAIL *dongaspar@sfol.com* WEBSITE *www.dongaspar.com*

LOCATION	From I-25, take the St. Francis exit and go 6 stoplights to Cordova. Turn right, go 2 stoplights to Galisteo, and turn left. Proceed to Paseo de Peralta (the first light), turn right, then right again onto Don Gaspar (at the first stoplight). The Compound is 1.5 blocks on the left (look for the coral adobe wall). Proceed to Booth Street, go left, then left again at the first driveway. Park in front of the adobe wall and walk through the gate on the left (look for the "office" sign). The office is straight ahead.
OPEN	All year
DESCRIPTION	A 1912 Mission and adobe inn with an adobe-walled garden courtyard and fountain. The inn is decorated with antiques and furnished in a Southwest style.
NO. OF ROOMS	All rooms with private bathrooms. Try the Courtyard Casita.
RATES	May through October, rates are $95-115 for a single or double, $145-175 for a suite, and $245 for the guesthouse. November through April, rates are $85-105 for a single or double, $115-145 for a suite, and $195 for the guesthouse. There is a minimum stay from May through October and cancellation requires 30 days' notice.
CREDIT CARDS	American Express, MasterCard, Visa
BREAKFAST	Continental plus is served in the dining room and includes cereals, yogurt, fruit, pastries, cheese, cold cuts, juices, coffees, teas, toast, bread, bagels, English muffins, and homemade jams.
AMENITIES	Robes; fresh coffee beans, grinder, and coffee-maker; microwave; toaster; refrigerator; teas, creamers, soda, and bottled water; turndown service; air conditioning; cable TV.
RESTRICTIONS	No smoking, no pets
REVIEWED	*Country Inns* magazine, *Frommer's*

MEMBER	Santa Fe Inns of Distinction, New Mexico Bed & Breakfast Association
AWARDS	1998, One of 1998's Top Affordable Luxury Inns in the United States, selected by *Country Inns* magazine
KUDOS/COMMENTS	"Charming southwestern estate with wonderful gardens about eight blocks from the Plaza." "Comfortable, clean, inviting urban setting, nice courtyard." (1996)

DOS CASAS VIEJAS

610 Agua Fria, Santa Fe, NM 87501 — *505-983-1636*
Susan & Michael Strijek, Resident Owners — *FAX 505-983-1749*
Some Spanish spoken
EMAIL doscasas@rt66.com
WEBSITE www.doscasasviejas.com

LOCATION	From I-25, take St. Francis Drive and go 3.8 miles, turning right at the Agua Fria intersection. The inn is 2 blocks on the right side.
OPEN	All year
DESCRIPTION	Six adobe casitas decorated with a mix of Native American, Anglo, and Spanish period furnishings in a secluded, walled compound on a gated half acre.
NO. OF ROOMS	Eight rooms with private bathrooms.
RATES	Year-round rates for a single or double are $185-195 and suites are $265. There is a minimum stay that varies. Cancellation requires 21 days' notice with a $25 charge.
CREDIT CARDS	MasterCard, Visa
BREAKFAST	Continental plus is served in the dining room, guestrooms, or on the poolside terrace and includes home-baked muffins, scones, and breads, Susie's sunshine cereal, fresh-squeezed orange juice, fresh fruit, yogurt, custom-blended coffee, and gourmet teas.
AMENITIES	All rooms feature private landscaped and furnished patios, wood-burning kiva fireplaces, original art, down pillows and comforters, cable TV, phones, and answering machines, CD player and stereos with CD library, bar refrigerators with bottled water, logo robes, plush towels, custom soaps, shampoos, and lotions; in-room spa services available; 40-foot heated lap pool with sunning/breakfast terrace; parking; concierge service; complimentary afternoon beverage service; some rooms with air conditioning; fax machine available; one room with handicapped access; bedside chocolates.
RESTRICTIONS	No smoking, no pets, children over 12 are welcome.

REVIEWED	*Travel & Leisure; The Insider's Guide to Santa Fe; Recommended Country Inns—The Southwest; Country Inns; America's Wonderful Little Hotels & Inns; Weekends for Two in the Southwest; Bed & Champagne—Top Romantic Hideaways; Fodor's The Southwest's Best Bed & Breakfasts; The Santa Fe & Taos Book*
RATED	AAA 3 Diamonds, ABBA 4 Crowns, Mobil 3 Stars
KUDOS/COMMENTS	"Gorgeous, if cost is no object I recommend it." "Excellent decor and lush amenities and the innkeepers are interesting. Private and very clean and done in good taste." (1996)

DUNSHEE'S

986 Acequia Madre, Santa Fe, NM 87501 *505-982-0988*
Susan Dunshee, Resident Owner
EMAIL *sdunshee@aol.com*
WEBSITE *www.bbhost.com/dunshee*

LOCATION	Proceed east on Canyon Road, then turn right on Camino del Monte Sol. Turn left at the first street, Acequia Madre, right at the second street, Martinez Lane, and proceed to the end of the dirt lane.
OPEN	All year
DESCRIPTION	A 1920s-era pueblo-style adobe and guesthouse. A secluded, traditional adobe compound, decorated with country furnishings and surrounded by gardens.
NO. OF ROOMS	Two rooms with private bathrooms.
RATES	Year-round rates are $125 for a suite or the guesthouse. There is a minimum stay on weekends and holidays and cancellation requires 10 days' notice.
CREDIT CARDS	MasterCard, Visa
BREAKFAST	Full gourmet breakfast is served in the suite. Serve-yourself continental plus stocked daily in the guesthouse kitchen and includes homemade muffins, granola, fruit, juice, yogurt, and coffee.
AMENITIES	Kiva fireplaces, fresh flowers, homemade cookies, folk art, antiques, TV, phone, CD player, coffee-maker, good books, private gardens and patios, mini-refrigerator, microwave. The guesthouse has a full kitchen.
RESTRICTIONS	No smoking. Dogs are allowed in the guesthouse with prior approval. The resident dogs are Roxie and Gracie.

REVIEWED — *Fodor's Santa Fe, Taos, Albuquerque; Fodor's The Southwest's Best Bed & Breakfasts; The Insider's Guide to Santa Fe, Taos, & Albuquerque; Adventure Guide to New Mexico; Romantic Days and Nights in Santa Fe; The Santa Fe & Taos Book; Hidden New Mexico; Ultimate Santa Fe and Beyond; Pets Welcome*

El Farolito Bed & Breakfast

514 Galisteo Street, Santa Fe, NM 87501 — *505-988-1631*
Walt Wyss, Innkeeper — *888-634-8782*
Spanish spoken — *FAX 505-988-4589*
EMAIL innkeeper@farolito.com — *WEBSITE www.farolito.com*

LOCATION	Take exit 282 off I-25 and head north on St. Francis Drive for several miles, turning right onto Cerillos Road. Drive 0.5 mile, turn right onto Paseo de Peralta, then go left onto Galisteo Street.
OPEN	All year
DESCRIPTION	Four adobe casitas in an off-street adobe compound with brick and tile floors, vigas and corbels, courtyards, and patios.
NO. OF ROOMS	Seven casitas with private bathrooms. Try the Acequia Madre.
RATES	May through October, rates are $130-150 for a single or double. December and January, rates are $95-120. February through April, rates are $110-145. There is a minimum stay when a Saturday night is involved and cancellation requires 14 days' notice with a $25 charge.
CREDIT CARDS	American Express, Discover, MasterCard, Visa

El Farolito Bed & Breakfast, Santa Fe

BREAKFAST	Continental plus is served in the dining room and includes home-baked goods, fresh fruit plate, French pastries, yogurt, juices, cereals, gourmet coffees, and teas. Special dietary needs are considered.
AMENITIES	All rooms have fireplaces with wood stocked daily during the burning season; all rooms are air conditioned and are decorated with original art and handcrafted furniture; four casitas have refrigerators; all have coffee service.
RESTRICTIONS	No smoking, no pets. C. J. is the resident dachshund.
REVIEWED	*Frommer's, Romantic Southwest, Compass American Guide—Santa Fe*
MEMBER	Professional Association of Innkeepers International, New Mexico Bed & Breakfast Association, New Mexico Hotel & Motel Association, Santa Fe Lodgers Association
RATED	AAA 3 Diamonds
KUDOS/COMMENTS	"Comfortable and attractive B&B in an ideal location." "Charming adobe casitas with original artwork." (1999)

El Paradero

220 West Manhattan, Santa Fe, NM 87501 *505-988-1177*
Ouida MacGregor & Thom Allen, Resident Owners
Spanish spoken
EMAIL *elpara@trail.com*
WEBSITE *www.elparadero.com*

LOCATION	From Highway 285 south, turn right on Paseo de Peralta and go south to Galisteo. Turn left on Galisteo and then left at the next corner (Manhattan). From Highway 285 north, take the second Paseo de Peralta exit (to state capitol), then take Paseo de Peralta left to Galisteo, et cetera.
OPEN	All year
DESCRIPTION	An eccentric 19th- and 20th-century rambling adobe plus a Victorian annex, with well-lit rooms and common space, located near the state capitol. Decorated with southwestern textiles and artwork.
NO. OF ROOMS	Twelve rooms with private bathrooms and two rooms share two bathrooms. Room 6 is the best room in the house.
RATES	May through October and major holidays a single or double with a private bathroom is $85-140, a single or double with a shared bathroom is $75-85, and a suite is $140. November through April, a single or double with a private bathroom is $75-125, a single or

double with a shared bathroom is $65-75, and a suite is $125. There is a three-day minimum stay on weekends, and cancellation requires seven days' notice with a $10 fee for reservations made with credit cards.

CREDIT CARDS MasterCard, Visa

BREAKFAST Full breakfast is served in the dining room and includes a daily main entrée such as huevos rancheros, banana-oatmeal pancakes, pesto eggs, blueberry-ricotta crepes, plus juice, fresh fruit, and home-baked goodies.

AMENITIES Tea time with baked goods, chips, salsa, tea, cider (winter); phones and air conditioning in each room; fireplaces in several rooms; piano in living room; champagne for special days.

RESTRICTIONS No smoking, dogs are allowed in some rooms with prior approval, children over two are welcome.

REVIEWED *Journey to the High Southwest; The Official Guide to American Historic Inns—Country Inns and Bed & Breakfasts; Fodor's Santa Fe, Taos, Albuquerque; On the Road; The Insider's Guide to Santa Fe; America's Wonderful Little Hotels & Inns; Backroads and Country Inns*

MEMBER Founding member of the New Mexico Bed & Breakfast Association and Santa Fe Bed & Breakfast Association, Professional Association of Innkeepers International

RATED AAA 3 Diamonds, Mobil 2 Stars

KUDOS/COMMENTS "One of the first B&Bs in New Mexico, El Paradero is friendly, comfortable and well-run by its very nice, hard-working owners." (1996)

Four Kachinas Inn

512 Webber Street, Santa Fe, NM 87501 *505-982-2550*
John Daw & Andrew Beckerman, Resident Owners *800-397-2564*
Some Spanish and some French spoken
EMAIL *info@fourkachinas.com*
WEBSITE *www.fourkachinas.com*

LOCATION Four-and-a-half blocks south of the Plaza.

OPEN All year except January

DESCRIPTION Northern New Mexico territorial inn built around a courtyard; furnished with tile floors, Native American art and Navajo rugs; renovated and added to in 1991.

NO. OF ROOMS Six rooms with private bathrooms.

RATES	April through October, rates are $87-149 for a single or double. November through March, rates are $75-125. High-season rates apply during major holidays. There is a two-night minimum stay on weekends and holidays and cancellation requires 14 days' notice.
CREDIT CARDS	Discover, MasterCard, Visa
BREAKFAST	Continental plus is served in the guestrooms and includes coffee, tea, orange juice, milk, yogurt, fruit, and fresh pastry. John is an award-winning baker.
AMENITIES	Afternoon tea with homemade cookies; wine for honeymooners, anniversaries, and return guests; ceiling fans, some private patios, woodstove in the library.
RESTRICTIONS	No smoking, no pets, children over 10 are welcome.
REVIEWED	*Fodor's Santa Fe, Taos, Albuquerque; Inn Places; Recommended Country Inns—The Southwest; Best Places to Stay in the Southwest*
MEMBER	New Mexico Bed & Breakfast Association, Professional Association of Innkeepers International
RATED	AAA 3 Diamonds
AWARDS	Three times awarded Best of Show, baking division, Santa Fe County Fair
KUDOS/COMMENTS	"Immaculately clean, good location, quiet but close to Plaza, spacious rooms." "Handsomely designed; good homemade breakfasts and welcoming hosts." (1996)

GRANT CORNER INN

122 Grant Avenue, Santa Fe, NM 87501 — *505-983-6678*
Louise Stewart, Resident Owner — *800-964-9003*
Spanish spoken — *FAX 505-983-1526*
EMAIL info@grantcornerinn.com
WEBSITE www.grantcornerinn.com

LOCATION	The inn is two blocks from the Plaza.
OPEN	All year
DESCRIPTION	A 1905 three-story colonial manor with a wraparound front porch and white pillars, decorated with traditional furnishings and antiques, and located in downtown Santa Fe.
NO. OF ROOMS	Ten rooms with private bathrooms and two rooms share one bathroom.

RATES	Please inquire about current rates and cancellation information.
CREDIT CARDS	American Express, MasterCard, Visa
BREAKFAST	Full gourmet breakfast is served in the dining room and includes fruit frappé, stuffed French toast, blue corn–blueberry pancakes, omelets, breakfast burritos. Breakfast in bed, lunch, picnic baskets, and holiday dinners are available.
AMENITIES	Homemade cookies in rooms, Sunday brunch with classical guitarist, fresh flowers, robes, wheelchair accessible, private phones, cable TV, air conditioning in the main inn, ceiling fans.
RESTRICTIONS	No smoking, no pets, children over eight are welcome.
REVIEWED	*The Insiders' Guide to Santa Fe; Journey to the High Southwest; Access Santa Fe, Taos & Albuquerque; New Mexico* magazine
MEMBER	Professional Association of Innkeepers International, Santa Fe Inns of Distinction
KUDOS/COMMENTS	"Excellent innkeeping, professional, clean, attractive Victorian. Wonderful breakfast." (1996) "All the hominess and charm of grandma's house right in the heart of town." (1999)

GUADALUPE INN

604 Agua Fria Street, Santa Fe, NM 87501 *505-989-7422*
Henrietta Quintana, Dolores Meyers, *FAX 505-989-7422*
& Pete Quintana, Resident Owners
Spanish spoken, sign language
WEBSITE www.guadalupeinn.com

LOCATION	Just over a half mile from downtown Santa Fe
OPEN	All year
DESCRIPTION	A 1992 two-story northern New Mexico inn with southwestern furnishings.
NO. OF ROOMS	Twelve rooms with private bathrooms.
RATES	April 15 to January 5, rates are $135-160 for a single or double and a suite is $185. January 6 to April 14, rates are $110-130 for a single or double and a suite is $150. There is a two-night minimum stay on weekends and four nights for Indian Market. Cancellation requires 10 days' notice.
CREDIT CARDS	American Express, Discover, MasterCard, Visa
BREAKFAST	Full breakfast is served in the dining room and includes coffee, juice, choice of two or three breads or muffins, eggs anyway you want them, huevos rancheros, breakfast burritos, or pancakes. Fruit plates are also available.

AMENITIES	Hot tub, meeting facilities, telephone, TV, air-conditioning, handicapped accessible, special requests filled with advance notice, on-site parking.
RESTRICTIONS	No smoking indoors, children are welcome with advance notice.
REVIEWED	*Recommended Country Inns—The Southwest; Best Places to Stay in the Southwest*
MEMBER	New Mexico Hotel and Motel Association

Hacienda Vargas Bed & Breakfast Inn

1431 El Camino Real (Hwy 313), Santa Fe, NM 87001 — *505-867-9115*
Paul DeVargas, Innkeeper — *800-261-0006*
Spanish and German spoken — *FAX 505-867-0640*
EMAIL hacvar@swcp.com — *WEBSITE www.swcp.com/hacvar*

LOCATION	From the Albuquerque airport, take I-25 north toward Santa Fe, get off on exit 248, and turn left (west). At the end of the road, turn left again (south) onto Highway 313, and go 0.5 mile. Look for the sign.
OPEN	All year
DESCRIPTION	An 1800s-era adobe hacienda with Spanish and Native American decor.
NO. OF ROOMS	Eight rooms with private bathrooms. Try the Kiva Suite.
RATES	Year-round rates are $60-89 for a single or double and $109-139 for a suite. There is a minimum stay during the Balloon Fiesta and cancellation requires 10 days' notice.
CREDIT CARDS	MasterCard, Visa
BREAKFAST	Full southwestern breakfast is served in the dining room or guestrooms and includes egg and side dishes, home-baked muffins, fresh fruit, orange juice, and coffee.
AMENITIES	Private courtyards, double Jacuzzis in suites, bubble bath, chocolate mints and candles, adobe chapel.
RESTRICTIONS	No smoking, no pets, children over 12 are welcome. Buddy and Josie are the resident pooches. "Smart and friendly, the dogs respect the area that guests frequent. We keep them by our quarters in the back. They never go inside the B&B."
REVIEWED	*Fodor's; Frommer's; Country Inn* magazine; *Recommended Country Inns—The Southwest*
MEMBER	New Mexico Bed & Breakfast Association, Albuquerque Bed & Breakfast Association, Innkeepers Association of New Mexico

RATED	AAA 3 Diamonds, Mobil 3 Stars
KUDOS/COMMENTS	"Authentic New Mexican atmosphere with professional and personable hosts." "Beautiful inn, gracious hosts, and very friendly, comfortable atmosphere." "Lovely old stagecoach stop, beautiful decor and great food. Friendly owners." (1996)

THE INN OF THE ANASAZI

113 Washington Avenue, Santa Fe, NM 87501 *505-988-3030*
WEBSITE www.innoftheanasazi.com

INN OF THE ANIMAL TRACKS

707 Paseo de Peralta, Santa Fe, NM 87501 *505-988-1546*
Allan & Myrna Wheeler, Innkeepers *FAX 505-982-8098*
EMAIL animal@trail.com *WEBSITE www.santafe.org/animaltracks*

LOCATION	From the Plaza, go two-and-a-half blocks on Palace Avenue, turn left (north) onto Paseo de Peralta, and go another half block.
OPEN	All year
DESCRIPTION	A turn-of-the-century Santa Fe inn with vigas, stucco, and handcarved trim, listed on the National and State Historic Registers. Each room is named and decorated after an animal.
NO. OF ROOMS	Five rooms with private bathrooms. Try the Deer Room.
RATES	Weekends from January 5 through June 14, rates are $90-130 for a single or double on the weekend. Weekends from June 15 through January 4, rates are $99-140 for a single or double. Midweek rates are less. There is a two-night minimum stay on weekends, three days during Indian Market and cancellation requires 14 days' notice.

Inn of the Animal Tracks, Santa Fe

CREDIT CARDS	American Express, MasterCard, Visa
BREAKFAST	Full breakfast is served in the dining room or on the secluded patio and includes fruit and juice, coffee, tea, and hot chocolate, followed by a breakfast burrito, waffles, and other freshly made goodies.
AMENITIES	Air conditioning, cable TV, phones, fax, kiva fireplace in living room and in one guestroom (Eagle Room), biggest teddy bear in Santa Fe, free parking, patio, library of Southwest information and literature.
RESTRICTIONS	No smoking, children and pets are welcome with prior approval.
REVIEWED	*Fodor's; Frommer's; 2 to 22 Days in the American Southwest; Compass American Guides; The Santa Fe & Taos Book*
MEMBER	New Mexico Bed & Breakfast Association

INN OF THE TURQUOISE BEAR—SANTA FE

342 E Buena Vista Street, Santa Fe, NM 87501 — *505-983-0798*
Robert Frost & Ralph Bolton, Innkeepers — *800-396-4104*
Spanish, French, German, and Norwegian spoken — *FAX 505-988-4225*
EMAIL bluebear@roadrunner.com — *WEBSITE www.turquoisebear.com*

LOCATION	From Albuquerque, take I-25 north for 55 miles. Take exit 284, Old Pecos Trail. At the stop sign, turn left, travel 1.5 miles, and turn right at the third signal, onto Old Pecos Trail. Continue for 1.2 miles through two signals. Old Pecos Trail merges with Old Santa Fe Trail after the second signal. Turn left on E. Buena Vista Street, 0.1 mile after the junction of Old Pecos Trail and Old Santa Fe Trail. Turn left into the first driveway. From Denver, head south on I-25 and take exit 284. Turn right, go 1.3 miles, and turn right again at the third signal. Then follow the above directions.
OPEN	All year
DESCRIPTION	A circa 1880 pueblo-style adobe inn with Southwest decor. Listed on the National and State Historic Registers.
NO. OF ROOMS	Eight rooms with private bathrooms and two rooms share two bathrooms. Try the Shaman Room.
RATES	April through October and holidays, rates are $100-195 for a single or double with a private bathroom, $95-135 for a single or double with a shared bathroom, and $250 for a suite. November through March, excluding holidays, rates are $100-175 for a single or double with a private bathroom, $95-120 for a single or double with a shared bathroom, and $225 for a suite. There is a minimum stay during some holidays and cancellation requires 14 days' notice with a $20 fee.

CREDIT CARDS	American Express, Discover, MasterCard, Visa
BREAKFAST	Continental plus is served in the dining room and includes home-baked breads, muffins, fresh-squeezed orange juice, sliced fruit, a selection of cereals, yogurt, gourmet coffee, and tea.
AMENITIES	Plush terry robes, cable TV/VCR, video library, book library, wine-and-cheese social hour, handicapped access to one room, small meeting facilities, fans, in-room phones with free local and 800 access, free firewood for fireplaces, off-street parking, concierge services.
RESTRICTIONS	No smoking. Spurs and Chaps are the resident cats. "Cats do not enter guest rooms, and they are kept out of public areas if an allergic guest is in house. They are mostly outdoor cats."
REVIEWED	*Hidden New Mexico; Fodor's Gay Guide to the USA; Pets Welcome*
MEMBER	New Mexico Hotel and Motel Association

Inn on the Alameda

303 East Alameda, Santa Fe, NM 87501 — *505-984-2121*
Elizabeth Colman, Manager — *800-289-2122*
WEBSITE www.inn-alameda.com — *FAX 505-986-8325*

Inn on the Paseo

630 Paseo de Peralta, Santa Fe, NM 87501 — *505-984-8200*
John & Lissa Hastings, Innkeepers — *800-457-9045*
A bit of Spanish spoken — *FAX 505-989-3979*
WEBSITE www.innonthepaseo.com

LOCATION	Four blocks northeast of the Plaza.
OPEN	All year
DESCRIPTION	Two northern New Mexico two-story homes have been conjoined by new construction. Decorated with colorful, contemporary southwestern furnishings.
NO. OF ROOMS	Eighteen rooms with private bathrooms.
RATES	Year-round rates are $75-135 for a single or double and $130-175 for a suite. Ask about minimum stay and cancellation information.
CREDIT CARDS	American Express, MasterCard, Visa

BREAKFAST	Continental plus buffet served in the dining room or on the deck in warm weather and includes homemade baked goods, regional specialties, cereals, fresh fruit, bagel basket, coffee, tea, and juice.
AMENITIES	Patchwork quilts, air conditioning in all rooms, cable TV with HBO, telephones, and one room is wheelchair accessible.
RESTRICTIONS	No smoking, no pets, children over 10 are welcome.
REVIEWED	*Berlitz; Fodor's*
MEMBER	Professional Association of Innkeepers International
RATED	Mobil 3 Stars

La Posada de Santa Fe

---

330 E Palace Avenue, Santa Fe, NM 87501 *800-727-5276*
WEBSITE www.laposadadesantafe.com

La Tienda Inn

445–447 W San Francisco Street, Santa Fe, NM 87501 *505-989-8259*
Leighton & Barbara Watson, Innkeepers *800-889-7611*
Some Spanish spoken *FAX 505-820-6931*
EMAIL info@latiendabb.com
WEBSITE www.latiendabb.com

LOCATION	Four blocks west of the Santa Fe Plaza.
OPEN	All year
DESCRIPTION	A 1900 walled adobe compound that includes a turn-of-the-century territorial-style house and a meandering adobe building, the front of which was built as a little neighborhood market, or tienda, with gardens and a fountain. Listed on the State Historic Register.
NO. OF ROOMS	Seven rooms with private bathrooms.
RATES	July, August, and holiday rates are $110-160 for a single or double. November and January through March, rates are $90-135 for a single or double. There is a minimum stay during weekends and holidays, and cancellation requires 14 days' notice.
CREDIT CARDS	MasterCard, Visa
BREAKFAST	Continental plus is served in the guestrooms or in the garden and includes an assortment of warm breads, fresh fruit salad, juice, yogurt, cereal, coffee, and tea.

AMENITIES	Afternoon tea, bottled water and fresh flowers in rooms, free parking, close to the Plaza, quiet and secluded, most rooms with air-conditioning and refrigerator, all with private entrances, private telephone lines, cable TV, three with fireplaces, handicapped accessible.
RESTRICTIONS	No smoking, no pets, children over 10 are welcome. Adolfo is the resident cat. "Adolfo is named for the man who built the old store, Adolfo Montoya, because he acts like he owns the place."
REVIEWED	*Frommer's Irreverent Guide to Santa Fe; Fodor's The Southwest's Best Bed & Breakfasts; The Insider's Guide to Santa Fe; National Trust Guide to Historic Bed & Breakfasts, Inns, and Small Hotels*
MEMBER	Santa Fe Inns of Distinction, New Mexico Bed & Breakfast Association, Professional Association of Innkeepers International
RATED	Mobil 3 Stars
AWARDS	Certificate of appreciation from Mayor Debbie Jaramillo for "sensitive renovation of 447 West San Francisco Street, a significant building in the Westside-Guadalupe Historic District."
KUDOS/COMMENTS	"Completely up to code for handicapped access, braille, etc., beautiful peaceful rooms, very tastefully done." (1996)

Open Sky

134 Turquoise Trail, Santa Fe, NM 87505 — *505-471-3475*
Babette Miller, Innkeeper — *800-244-3475*
German and Spanish spoken — *FAX 505-474-6493*
EMAIL SkyMiller@AOL.com — *WEBSITE www.OpenSkyNM.com*

LOCATION	Seven miles south of Santa Fe off Highway 14, the Turquoise Trail, a 10-minute drive from I-25. Sixteen miles from the Plaza in Santa Fe.
OPEN	All year
DESCRIPTION	A 1977 adobe inn with high viga ceilings, spacious rooms, many patios, and 360-degree views of the Jemez, Oriz, and Sangre de Cristo mountain ranges.
NO. OF ROOMS	Four rooms with private bathrooms.
RATES	Year-round rates are $70-120 for a single or double. There is a minimum stay on weekends and cancellation requires two weeks' notice.
CREDIT CARDS	Discover, MasterCard, Visa
BREAKFAST	Continental plus is served in the guestrooms or at private tables and includes fresh breads, fruit, breakfast parfaits, muffins, or French toast with raspberry sauce. "Some breakfasts are hot, some are not."

AMENITIES	Large living area for group meetings, handicapped-accessible room, outdoor Jacuzzi, horseback riding, hiking, massage, astrology and tarot readings.
RESTRICTIONS	No smoking. Jessie is the resident pooch and there are three cats: Blue, Spaxton, and Krishna.
REVIEWED	*Fodor's; Ferrari Guide; Pets Welcome; Damron Accommodations*

PRESTON HOUSE

106 Faithway Street, Santa Fe, NM 87501 — *505-982-3465*
Andrea Corchran, Manager — *FAX 505-982-3465*

KUDOS/COMMENTS	"Very nice, clean, comfortable Victorian home in downtown Santa Fe. Good breakfast." "The quiet elegance and charm of the 'Old' Santa Fe. Great neighborhood as well." (1996)

PUEBLO BONITO BED & BREAKFAST INN

138 West Manhattan Avenue, Santa Fe, NM 87501 — *505-984-8001*
Herb & Amy Behm, Owners — *FAX 505-984-3155*

RANCHO ENCANTADO

RR 4, Box 57, Santa Fe, NM 87501 — *505-982-353*

RANCHO JACONA

Route 5, Box 250, Santa Fe, NM 87501 — *505-455-7948*

SANTA FE BUDGET PENSION

1416 Cerrillos Road, Santa Fe, NM 87505 — *505-988-1153*
WEBSITE *www.santa-fe.net/sfih*

The Spencer House Bed & Breakfast Inn

222 McKenzie, Santa Fe, NM 87501 — *505-988-3024*
Jan McConnell, Innkeeper — *800-647-0530*
WEBSITE www.spencerhse-santafe.com

LOCATION	From I-25, take Route 285 north for 3 miles, turn right onto Cerrillos Road, and drive to the first stoplight. Go left on Guadalupe, drive past 4 stoplights, and take a right on McKenzie.
OPEN	All year
DESCRIPTION	A 1923 Mediterranean-style adobe cottage decorated with antiques, located 4 blocks from the Plaza and just around the corner from the Georgia O'Keeffe museum.
NO. OF ROOMS	Five rooms with private bathrooms.
RATES	May through October, rates are $105-135 for a single or double and $150 for the guesthouse. November through April, rates are $95-125 for a single or double and $140 for the guesthouse. There is a minimum stay during weekends and major holidays.
CREDIT CARDS	American Express, MasterCard, Visa
BREAKFAST	Full breakfast is served in the dining room and includes fresh-squeezed orange juice, fresh fruit, yogurt, homemade granola, cereals, and a hot dish such as pancakes, waffles, French toast, eggs, bacon, and sausage. Special dietary needs are accommodated.
AMENITIES	Air conditioning, bottled water and sparkling water, cookies, biscotti, cakes, chocolates.
RESTRICTIONS	No smoking, no pets, children over 12 are welcome.
REVIEWED	*Frommer's; Best Places to Stay in the Southwest; Recommended Country Inns—The Southwest; America's Wonderful Little Hotels & Inns; The Complete Guide to Bed & Breakfasts, Inns & Guesthouses in the United States, Canada, and Worldwide*
MEMBER	New Mexico Bed & Breakfast Association, Professional Association of Innkeepers International
RATED	AAA 3 Diamonds, Mobil 2 Stars
AWARDS	1993, Historical Restoration Award
KUDOS/COMMENTS	"Beautifully decorated, small inn near the center of town. Immaculately clean with a lovely little garden." "Charming, country-style inn near the plaza." "Clean, cozy, beautifully furnished, welcoming atmosphere." (1996)

Territorial Inn

215 Washington Avenue, Santa Fe, NM 87501 *505-989-7737*
WEBSITE *www.territorialinn.com*

Triangle Inn

PO Box 3235, Sante Fe, NM 87501 *505-455-3375*
WEBSITE *www.triangleinn.com*

Vistas de los Pueblos

47 Feather Road, Santa Fe, NM 87501 *505-455-3635*

Water Street Inn

427 West Water Street, Santa Fe, NM 87501 *505-984-1193*

KUDOS/COMMENTS "A beautifully restored adobe in downtown Santa Fe. Friendly staff, comfortably luxurious." (1996)

Santa Teresa

The gateway to Big Bend National Park, Santa Teresa lies near Juarez, Mexico, and four of the oldest missions in the United States. The Mexican food here is unrivaled.

Cowboys & Indians Bed & Breakfast

405 Mountain Vista, Santa Teresa, NM 88008 *505-589-2653*
Don & Irene Newlon, Innkeepers *FAX 505-589-4512*
Some Spanish spoken

LOCATION	Take I-10 west to the Artcraft exit and go west. Take a right at Doniphan, left at Farm Road 128, right at Koogle, and left at Mt. Vista. Drive to the top of the hill.
OPEN	All year
DESCRIPTION	A 1995 adobe hacienda decorated with Old West and Native American furnishings and antiques, situated on a mesa overlooking the Franklin Mountains and the lights of El Paso.
NO. OF ROOMS	Four rooms with private bathrooms. Try Pocahantas Palace.
RATES	Year-round rates are $67-97 for a single or double. There is no minimum stay and cancellation requires 24 hours' notice.
CREDIT CARDS	American Express, Diners Club, MasterCard, Visa
BREAKFAST	Full breakfast is served in the dining room and features chuckwagon and southwestern cuisine, including vegetables and fruits from local farms and orchards.
AMENITIES	Robes, southwestern snacks, coffee-makers, private patios, individual air conditioning units, phones, one room handicapped accessible, one room with massage bed, TV available.
RESTRICTIONS	No smoking, no pets, children over 10 are welcome. Skimmer is the resident pooch.
RATED	Mobil 3 Stars

SILVER CITY

This classic Victorian mining town, perched at 6,000 feet at the edge of the Pinos Altos Mountains, is the western gateway to the 3.3 million-acre Gila Wilderness. Explore Gila Cliff Dwellings National Monument and City of Rocks State Park, and take the catwalk in Whitewater Canyon. Silver City is also home to Western New Mexico University. About 50 miles north of Deming on scenic Highway 180.

THE CARTER HOUSE

101 North Cooper Street, Silver City, NM 88061 *505-388-5485*
Lucy Dilworth, Resident Owner

LOCATION	Next door to the Grant County Courthouse, on the edge of Silver City's historic district.
OPEN	All year
DESCRIPTION	A 1906 three-story Queen Anne colonial revival with an ornate interior and eclectic mix of antiques and mission furnishings.

The Carter House, Silver City

NO. OF ROOMS	Five rooms with private bathrooms. Try the Crow Canyon Room.
RATES	Year-round rates for a single or double are $57-75. There is a minimum stay on major holiday weekends and cancellation requires seven days' notice.
CREDIT CARDS	American Express, MasterCard, Visa
BREAKFAST	Full breakfast is served in the dining room and includes two types of juice, fresh fruit, muffins or sweet bread, yeasted bread, cereals, hot beverage, eggs and meats cooked to order; on some days pancakes, French toast, or quiche are included.
AMENITIES	Homebaked cookies with tea anytime, huge covered front porch with a view of the mountains, hostel downstairs with laundry facilities and soda machine.
RESTRICTIONS	No smoking, no pets. Bill is the resident Lab/collie mix.
REVIEWED	*America's Wonderful Little Hotels & Inns; Off the Beaten Path—New Mexico; The Birder's Guide to Bed & Breakfasts; Frommer's; Let's Go USA*
MEMBER	New Mexico Bed & Breakfast Association.
RATED	AAA 3 Diamonds
AWARDS	1995, Ruth & Bill Nelson Award, American Youth Hostels

The Cottages

2037 Cottage San Road, Silver City, NM 88062 *505-388-3000*
Mike & Callahan, Innkeepers *800-938-3001*
WEBSITE www.zianet.com/cottages

LOCATION	Six-and-a-half blocks north of Highway 180. Look for the private, gated driveway.
OPEN	All year
DESCRIPTION	Secluded 1930s-era country French cottages nestled in a virgin forest on the slopes of the Continental Divide, at the edge of the Gila Wilderness.
NO. OF ROOMS	Cottages with private bathrooms.
RATES	Year-round rates are $89-199. There is a two-night minimum stay year-round and cancellation requires 72 hours' notice.
CREDIT CARDS	American Express, Discover, MasterCard, Visa
BREAKFAST	Full breakfast is served in the cottages and includes fresh fruit, juices, bacon, eggs, sausage, pancakes, waffles, yogurt, gourmet coffees, teas, hot chocolate, hot or cold cereals, muffins, toast, bagels, and more.
AMENITIES	Cottages have their own private settings, with full kitchens, living rooms with wood-burning fireplaces, VCRs, phones, and air conditioning, hot mineral baths, luxurious feather beds.
RESTRICTIONS	No smoking inside cottages, no pets, no children.

La Posada de Tierra Alta

114 S Cooper Street, Silver City, NM 88061 *505-534-2782*
WEBSITE www.tierra-alta.com

Palace Hotel

106 West Broadway, Silver City, NM 88061 — *505-388-1811*
Cal & Nancy Thompson, Resident Owners — *FAX 505-388-1811*
Spanish spoken
WEBSITE www.zianet.com/palacehotel

LOCATION	Downtown at the intersection of Bullard and Broadway, in the center of the historic downtown.
OPEN	All year
DESCRIPTION	A restored 1882 two-story Victorian–art deco hotel with Victorian and eclectic furnishings.
NO. OF ROOMS	Eighteen rooms with private bathrooms and one room shares one bathroom.
RATES	Year-round rates for a single or double with a private bathroom are $29.50-48, the room with the shared bathroom is $26.50, and the suite is $48. There is no minimum stay and cancellation requires 24 hours' notice.
CREDIT CARDS	American Express, Diners Club, Discover, MasterCard, Visa
BREAKFAST	Continental breakfast is served in the upstairs lobby and includes assorted breads, cream cheese, jam, fruit, juice, coffee, and tea.
AMENITIES	Cable TV, telephones, guest use of microwave and refrigerator, refrigerators in suites, steam heat.

The Palace Hotel, Silver City

RESTRICTIONS	No pets, smoking OK in some rooms
REVIEWED	*Frommer's New Mexico; Fodor's; Frommer's America on Wheels Southwest; Berlitz; Let's Go USA.; Lonely Planet*
AWARDS	1991, New Mexico Historic Preservation Society Award; 1991, Heritage Historic Preservation Award

Socorro

Casa Blanca B&B Guesthouse

13 Montoya Street, San Antonio, NM 87828 — *505-835-3027*

Springer

In the northeast of the state, 58 miles south of the Colorado border on I-25. Visit the Santa Fe Trail Museum in the old Colfax County Courthouse. Kiowa National Grasslands are just to the southeast.

The Brown Hotel

302 Maxwell Avenue, Springer, NM 87747 — *505-483-2269*
Roy & Debbie Ackerman, Resident Owners — *800-570-2269*
Spanish spoken — *505-483-0053*

LOCATION	In the town of Springer, 1 mile from exit 412 on I-25.
OPEN	All year
DESCRIPTION	A 1921 two-story hotel with early 1920s furniture. The owners have applied for inclusion of the hotel on the State Historic Register.
NO. OF ROOMS	Eleven rooms share four bathrooms.
RATES	Year-round rates for a single or double are $40-70. There is no minimum stay and cancellation requires 24 hours' notice.
CREDIT CARDS	MasterCard, Visa
BREAKFAST	Full breakfast is served and includes eggs any style, pancakes, breakfast burritos, omelets, huevos rancheros, hash browns, homemade bread, fresh doughnuts, turnovers, muffins and cinnamon rolls made in our bakery. Lunch, dinner, and special meals are available on request. The hotels also caters to groups.

AMENITIES	The shared bathrooms have old-style pedestal bathtubs, all the rooms are furnished with antiques.
RESTRICTIONS	No smoking, no pets
REVIEWED	*New Mexico* magazine

TAOS

Taos bubbles over with history and events that celebrate its rich and colorful past—and it has arguably wrested from Santa Fe the title of the Southwest's quintessential art and literary center. Explore Taos Pueblo, the historic plaza, Martinez Hacienda, the Millicent Rogers Museum, and Spanish missions. Local festivals and events include San Geronimo Days, Wool Festival, Talking Picture Festival, Spring and Fall Arts Festivals, and Wine Festival. Taos Ski Valley is just up the road. Nestled against the mountains, 80 miles north of Santa Fe via Highways 285 and 68.

ABOMINABLE SNOW MANSION

476 Ski Valley Road (Highway 150), Taos, NM 87571 — *505-776-8298*
EMAIL snowman@newmex.com — *FAX 505-776-2107*
WEBSITE www.taoswebb.com/hotel/snowmansion

LOCATION	Nine miles from the ski valley.
OPEN	Mid-November through mid-April
NO. OF ROOMS	Five rooms with private bathrooms and three dormitories.
RATES	Please inquire about current rates and cancellation information.
CREDIT CARDS	Discover, MasterCard, Visa
BREAKFAST	Full breakfast is served in the dining room.

ADOBE & PINES INN

Highway 68, Ranchos de Taos, NM 87557 — *505-751-0947*
Chuck Fulkerson, Innkeeper — *800-723-8267*
WEBSITE www.taosnet.com/adobepines/ — *FAX 505-758-8423*

KUDOS/COMMENTS "Quaint, small, friendly country atmosphere."

Adobe and Stars Bed & Breakfast Inn

584 State Highway 150, Taos, NM 87571 — *505-776-2776*
Judy Salathiel, Innkeeper — *800-211-7076*
Spanish spoken — *FAX 505-776-2872*
EMAIL stars@taos.newmex.com — *WEBSITE www.taosadobe.com*

LOCATION	Ten miles from the Taos Plaza, 6 miles north of the intersection of Highways 64 and 150 (Ski Valley Road).
OPEN	All year
DESCRIPTION	A 1996 two-story southwestern adobe-style inn with Southwest decor, set in the foothills of the Sangre de Cristos at the entrance to Taos Ski Valley Canyon and Carson National Forest, with panoramic mountain views.
NO. OF ROOMS	Eight rooms with private bathrooms.
RATES	Year-round rates are $90-180 for a single or double and $320 for a suite. There is a minimum stay during holidays and cancellation requires 14 days' notice, 30 days during Christmas.
CREDIT CARDS	American Express, Discover, MasterCard, Visa
BREAKFAST	Full breakfast is served in the dining room or guestrooms.
AMENITIES	Afternoon snacks, robes, wine and hors d'oeuvres, handicapped accessible.
RESTRICTIONS	No smoking. Children are welcome. Maggie is the resident cat.
MEMBER	New Mexico Bed & Breakfast Association, Taos Bed & Breakfast Association, Traditional Taos Inns, Taos Association of Bed & Breakfast Inns
RATED	AAA 3 Diamonds, Mobile 3 Stars

Alma del Monte-Spirit of the Mountain B&B

372 Hondo Seco Road, Taos, NM 87571 — *505-776-2721*
Suzanne S. Head, Innkeeper — *800-273-7303*
Spanish spoken — *FAX 505-776-8888*
EMAIL suzanneh@newmex.com
WEBSITE www.AlmaDelMonteB-B.com/spirit/

LOCATION	Take Highway 64 north for about 4 miles to Highway 150. Turn right and travel 2.5 miles. Turn left onto Highway 230, drive 1.9 miles, turn left onto B143, and drive 0.5 mile, to the sign on the left.

OPEN	All year
DESCRIPTION	A 1995 one-and-a-half-story adobe hacienda with eclectic Southwest decor, with panoramic vistas of mountains and mesas.
NO. OF ROOMS	Five rooms with private bathrooms. Suzanne recommends Hank's Room.
RATES	Year-round rates are $135-250 for a single or double. There is a minimum stay during holidays and cancellation requires 14 days' notice with a 10 percent charge.
CREDIT CARDS	American Express, MasterCard, Visa
BREAKFAST	Full gourmet breakfast is served buffet style in the dining room and includes three or four juices, a separate fruit plate, and a full entrée.
AMENITIES	Guest refrigerators stocked with complimentary sodas and wines, a snack drawer, a tea and beverage drawer with an instant hot water dispenser, usually flowers or champagne for the honeymooners' guestrooms, files containing information about hikes and activities always available, a multitude of games, courtyard garden with fountain and hammocks, private garden with mountain and mesa vistas, stargazing.
RESTRICTIONS	No smoking, no pets, children over 16 are welcome. Tigglette is the cat; Fetchin' Lord Stanley is the chocolate Lab. "Stanley will take any guest for a walk or hike, and show off his pond and friends, like Bucky, a pet donkey, or the llamas, etc."
REVIEWED	*Frommer's Santa Fe, Taos, & Albuquerque; The Santa Fe and Taos Book; Romantic Days and Nights in Santa Fe; Santa Fe–Taos Handbook— Including Albuquerque*
MEMBER	Professional Association of Innkeepers International, Taos Bed & Breakfast Association, Taos Association of Bed & Breakfast Inns, New Mexico Bed & Breakfast Association
AWARDS	1997, New Inn of the Month, Inn Marketing

American Artists Gallery House Bed & Breakfast Inn

132 Frontier Road, Taos, NM 87571 — *505-758-4446*
LeAn & Charles Clamurro, Resident Owners — *800-532-2041*
EMAIL *aagh@taosnm.com* — *FAX 505-758-0497*
WEBSITE *www.taosbedandbreakfast.com*

LOCATION	From the Plaza, go 0.9 mile south, turn left onto Frontier Lane, just past the Ramada Inn and before Polson-Mercer Inn. The inn is at the end of Frontier Lane on the right.

OPEN	All year
DESCRIPTION	A 1950s adobe hacienda and casita with southwestern and a touch of country furnishings.
NO. OF ROOMS	Ten rooms with private bathrooms. Pick one of the Jacuzzi suites.
RATES	Please inquire about current rates and cancellation information.
CREDIT CARDS	MasterCard, Visa
BREAKFAST	Full gourmet breakfast is served in the dining room and includes in-season fresh fruits and vegetables prepared in a southwestern style.
AMENITIES	Outdoor hot tub, robes, afternoon refreshments, stocked guest refrigerator with homemade Tollhouse cookies, lemonade, sun tea, and bottled water. All rooms have woodburning kiva fireplaces.
RESTRICTIONS	No smoking, no pets, inquire about children.
REVIEWED	*Fodor's Southwest; Recommended Country Inns—The Southwest; Best Places to Stay in the Southwest; America's Wonderful Little Hotels and Inns; Journey to the High Southwest*
MEMBER	Taos Bed & Breakfast Association, New Mexico Bed & Breakfast Association, Professional Association of Innkeepers International
KUDOS/COMMENTS	"Great innkeepers, lovely suites, wonderful breakfasts."

AMIZETTE INN

1295 Highway 150, Taos Ski Valley, NM 87525 — *505-776-2451*
Richard & Vicky Maxwell, Innkeepers — *800-446-8267*
505-776-2451

DESCRIPTION	A rustic, 100-year-old mountain lodge overlooking the Rio Hondo.
NO. OF ROOMS	Ten rooms with private bathrooms.
RATES	Please inquire about current rates and cancellation information.
CREDIT CARDS	Discover, MasterCard, Visa
AMENITIES	All rooms have telephones and TVs; hot tub and sauna; will book horseback rides and river-rafting excursions; all rooms overlook the Rio Hondo.
RESTRICTIONS	No smoking, no pets, children under 5 stay free.

Blueberry Hill Bed & Breakfast

03 Margarita Lane, Taos, NM 87571 *505-758-8553*
Edward & Victoria Trujillo Ramsey, Innkeepers *FAX 505-758-5298*
Spanish spoken
EMAIL info@taosbbhill.com
WEBSITE www.taosbbhill.com

LOCATION	From the southwest corner of Taos Plaza in the center of town, drive west 3.4 miles on Highway 240 (Ranchitos Road). Go through a tight S-curve, pass the Martinez Hacienda, and go through another tight S-curve. At 3.4 miles, turn onto Blueberry Hill Road, a sharp right turn uphill. The B&B is 1.4 miles up on the right.
OPEN	All year
DESCRIPTION	A 1976 two-and-a-half-story pueblo-style country inn with a split-level solar orientation with Spanish colonial furnishings, saltillo tile, hand-adzed beams, antiques, fine art, and crafts. The inn offers beautiful panoramic views.
NO. OF ROOMS	Five rooms with private bathrooms.
RATES	Year-round rates are $60-70 for a single or double, $140 for a suite, and $125 for the apartment. There is no minimum stay and cancellation requires 10 days' notice with a $10 fee.
CREDIT CARDS	No
BREAKFAST	Full gourmet breakfast is served in the dining room and features southwestern and house specialties. "Only the freshest fruit and ingredients are used."
AMENITIES	Panoramic views (up to 100 miles) in all directions, sunken greenhouse, Jacuzzi tubs, beautiful custom tilework in all baths, flagstone patios, second-story decks, plant-filled atrium, satellite TV/VCRs, year-round gardens, jewelry studio, apartment with kitchen facilities and fenced yard.
RESTRICTIONS	No smoking, no pets. Ask about children. Bo is the resident Pomeranian, Ally is the shepherd mix, and Bluesette is the blue heeler mix.

Brooks Street Inn Bed & Breakfast

119 Brooks Street, Taos, NM 87571 — *505-758-1489*
Carol Frank, Innkeeper — *800-758-1489*
Spanish spoken
EMAIL brooks@taos.newmex.com
WEBSITE www.brooksstreetinn.com

LOCATION Three blocks north of the Taos Plaza and the center of town. Brooks Street is one long block. The inn is located near the end of the block, on the north side of the street.

OPEN All year

DESCRIPTION A 1954 adobe territorial inn and a pueblo-style guesthouse with a walled courtyard and garden. The inn and guesthouse are furnished in a Southwest style, with locally crafted furniture and fine artwork from local artists. The main home has shiny pine floors and wood-beamed ceilings; the guesthouse features saltillo tiled floors and kiva fireplaces.

NO. OF ROOMS Six rooms with private bathrooms. Try the Juniper Room.

RATES Year-round rates are $80-110 for a single or double, except during Christmas holidays when they are slightly higher. There is a minimum stay during Christmas holidays, special events, and weekends. Cancellation requires 10 days' notice with a $15 fee.

CREDIT CARDS American Express, MasterCard, Visa

BREAKFAST Full gourmet breakfast is served in the dining room or garden in the summer and includes blue-corn pancakes served with a fresh pineapple salsa, white chocolate apricot scones, a ricotta and cream-cheese blintz soufflé topped with black cherry compote, or stuffed French toast drizzled with apricot glaze. Fresh fruits, juices, organic granolas, and specialty coffees are always available.

AMENITIES All rooms with coffee-makers, coffee, teas, and hot chocolate, clock radios, robes, shampoo, lotion, and glycerine soaps; hair dryers available; each room has fresh flowers; some rooms have fireplaces, reading nooks, refrigerators, and CD players; snacks, coffee, tea, and other non-alcoholic beverages provided; concierge services; a hammock for two; noted Taos artists frequently join guests during breakfast as part of a "Meet the Artist" program.

RESTRICTIONS No smoking, no pets. Brooks is the resident golden retriever, Gracie is the black Lab, and Amy the cat. "Brooks and Gracie are the official greeters. Brooks loves to eat ice and bananas!"

REVIEWED *Fodor's Santa Fe, Taos, Albuquerque; Frommer's Santa Fe, Taos & Albuquerque; The Santa Fe & Taos Book; Best Places to Stay in the Southwest; The Complete Guide to Bed & Breakfasts, Inns and Guesthouses in the United States, Canada, and Worldwide; You Are Cordially Invited to the Best Choices in New Mexico; America's Wonderful Little Hotels & Inns*

MEMBER	Professional Association of Innkeepers International, Taos Association of Bed & Breakfasts, New Mexico Bed & Breakfast Association
RATED	AAA 3 Diamonds, Mobil 3 Stars
AWARDS	1988, Top Ten Inns, *Country Inns*

CASA BENAVIDES

137 Kit Carson Road, Taos, NM 87571 *505-758-1772*
WEBSITE www.taosnet.com/casabena/

KUDOS/COMMENTS	"Charming southwestern decor, excellent hospitality and food, convenient location."

CASA DE LAS CHIMENEAS BED & BREAKFAST INN

405 Cordoba Road, Taos, NM 87571 *505-758-4777*
Susan Vernon, Resident Owner
Some Spanish and some Italian spoken *FAX 505-758-3976*
EMAIL casa@newmex.com *WEBSITE www.Visit-Taos.com*

LOCATION	From the south (Santa Fe), turn right on Los Pandos off Paseo del Pueblo Sur (Highway 68), go 1 block, and turn right on Cordoba at the four-way stop. The inn is 4 blocks from the Plaza.
OPEN	All year
DESCRIPTION	A 1910 New Mexico territorial inn with multiple recent additions and southwestern furnishings.
NO. OF ROOMS	Eight rooms with private bathrooms.
RATES	Year-round rates for a single or double are $140-235 and $170-450 for suites. Christmas rates are higher. There is no minimum stay and cancellation requires 10 days' notice, 14 days during ski season, 30 days during Christmas.
CREDIT CARDS	American Express, MasterCard, Visa
BREAKFAST	Full breakfast is served in the dining room or guestrooms and includes a fruit course such as baked pears in a pastry crust served with fruit frappé, coffee and teas, followed by a hot entrée such as breakfast burritos, French toast, or artichoke and three-cheese omelet.

AMENITIES	Hors d'oeuvres; minibars in rooms stocked with complimentary soft drinks, juices, and mineral water; in-room kettles with coffee and tea; robes; fireplaces; outdoor hot tub; fitness facility with workout room and sauna; on-site massage and spa treatment center.
RESTRICTIONS	No smoking, no pets
REVIEWED	*Fodor's Santa Fe, Taos, Albuquerque; Frommer's Santa Fe, Taos & Albuquerque; Recommended Country Inns—The Southwest; America's Wonderful Little Hotels & Inns; Best Places to Stay in the Southwest; Access Santa Fe, Taos, & Albuquerque; Country Inns & Backroads—North America; Journey to the High Southwest*
MEMBER	Taos Bed & Breakfast Association, New Mexico Bed & Breakfast Association, Professional Association of Innkeepers International
RATED	AAA 3 Diamonds, Mobil 3 Stars
KUDOS/COMMENTS	"The B&B to stay at for five-star treatment in Taos." "A luxurious slice of perfection."

CASA ENCANTADA

416 Leibert Street, Taos, NM 87571 — *505-758-7477*
WEBSITE *www.casaencantada.com*

CASA EUROPA INN & GALLERY

840 Upper Ranchitos Road, Taos, NM 87571 — *505-758-9798*
Rudi & Marcia Zwicker, Resident Owners — *888-758-9798*
Spanish and German spoken — *FAX 505-758-9798*
EMAIL *casa-europa@travelbase.com*
WEBSITE *www.travelbase.com/destinations/taos/casa-europa/*

LOCATION	South of the Plaza on Highway 68, at the light by McDonalds, turn west on Placitas Road and go 1 block to the three-way stop. Turn west on State Road 240 (Ranchitos Road), go 1.3 miles, turn right on Upper Ranchitos Road and go 0.3 mile.
OPEN	All year
DESCRIPTION	A 1700s-era two-story territorial adobe with enclosed courtyards in a country setting with views. The furnishings are a mix of southwestern and European antiques.
NO. OF ROOMS	Seven rooms with private bathrooms.

RATES	Year-round rates for a single or double are $85-165 and the suites rent for $105-165. Christmas rates are higher. There is no minimum stay and cancellation requires 14 days' notice.
CREDIT CARDS	American Express, MasterCard, Visa
BREAKFAST	Full breakfast is served in the dining room and includes fresh fruit or juice, and an entrée such as chili relleno omelet, eggs Benedict, or a non-egg dish such as piñon waffles.
AMENITIES	European pastries in afternoons (except during ski season), evening hors d'oeuvres, two rooms have private hot tubs, outside hot tub and sauna in the back courtyard, robes, and in-house massage.
RESTRICTIONS	No smoking inside the casa. There are numerous dogs, cats, and horses, including Jose, Whiskers, Gabby, Trouble, Bebe, Grey, Buster, Papa, Hug Me Easy.
REVIEWED	*Fodor's; Frommer's; Recommended Country Inns—The Southwest; America's Wonderful Little Hotels & Inns*
MEMBER	New Mexico Bed & Breakfast Association, American Bed & Breakfast Association, Taos Bed & Breakfast Association

Casa Grande Guest Ranch B&B

75 Luis O. Torres Road, Arroyo Seco, NM 87514 — *505-776-1303*
Fran & Joe Torres, Innkeepers — *888-236-1303*
Spanish spoken — *FAX 505-776-2177*
EMAIL *cggr@newmex.com* — WEBSITE *www.guestranch.com*

LOCATION	From the historic Taos Plaza, go north 4 miles on Highway 68. At the stoplight, turn right onto Highway 150 and head toward Taos Ski Valley. Continue on Highway 150 for 5 miles to Arroyo Seco. When you reach the community center, proceed straight up El Salto Road for 1.1 miles. Turn left onto Luis O. Torres Road and drive 0.7 mile, staying left until you reach the B&B.
OPEN	All year
DESCRIPTION	A 1992 two-story contemporary adobe inn with Southwest decor and Spanish accents, nestled in the foothills of the El Salto Mountains.
NO. OF ROOMS	Three rooms with private bathrooms. Try the Sunrise Room.
RATES	Year-round rates are $125-195 for a single or double. There is a minimum stay on weekends and during holidays, and cancellation requires 14 days' notice and a 15 percent charge.
CREDIT CARDS	American Express, MasterCard, Visa

BREAKFAST	Full deluxe breakfast is served in the dining room or on the patio and includes regional entrées such as Fran's signature breakfast burrito with homemade salsa, baked goods, juice, coffee, tea, and fresh fruit.
AMENITIES	Each room has fresh flowers, robes, iron and ironing board, clock radio, hair dryer, hot tub, towels, reading lights, full-length mirrors, and spectacular views; the ranch features an indoor exercise room, outdoor hot tub surrounded by a 1,000-square-foot garden and majestic views; afternoon refreshments; horse boarding; horseback riding at an extra cost.
RESTRICTIONS	No smoking, no pets. There are cattle, bison, and a variety of horses on the property.
MEMBER	Association of Taos Bed & Breakfast Inns, Professional Association of Innkeepers International

Casa Nacoma

25 Nacoma Road, Taos, NM 87571 — *505-776-2267*
Donne Whisenand, Resident Owner

Cottonwood Inn

2 State Route 230, Taos, NM 87514 — *505-776-5826*
Kit & Bill Owen, Innkeepers — *800-324-7120*
Spanish and German spoken — *FAX 505-776-114*
EMAIL cottonbb@taosnewmex.com — *WEBSITE www.taos-cottonwood.com*

LOCATION	Drive 4 miles north of Taos to State Road 150, then go east exactly 2.5 miles to State Road 230 and turn left.
OPEN	All year
DESCRIPTION	A 1947 two-story pueblo-style adobe inn set on 1 acre of extensive perennial gardens and a grove of cottonwoods.
NO. OF ROOMS	Seven rooms with private bathrooms. Try the Mesa Vista Room.
RATES	Year-round rates are $85-155 for a single or double. There is a minimum stay during holidays and cancellation requires 14 days' notice for a full refund.
CREDIT CARDS	Discover, MasterCard, Visa

BREAKFAST Full breakfast is served in the dining room or on the patio in summer and includes a hot entrée such as blueberry blintz soufflé, veggie frittata with wine and herbs, pecan French toast, salmon quiche, plus fresh fruit and homemade baked goods. A special Thanksgiving dinner is also prepared.

AMENITIES Handicapped accessible, evening hors d'oeuvres, walking and running trail, discount on ski-lift tickets, maps and information to area outdoor recreation options, stargazing through the telescope.

RESTRICTIONS No smoking inside, no pets, children are welcome. Pugly, Gracey, and Matilda are the resident cats; Henny Penny, Goldie, and Chicken Little are the pet chickens.

REVIEWED *Frommer's Santa Fe, Taos, & Albuquerque; Fodor's The Southwest's Best Bed & Breakfasts; Off the Beaten Path—New Mexico; New Mexico Handbook*

MEMBER Association of Taos Bed & Breakfast Inns, Traditional Taos Inns Association, Taos Bed & Breakfast Association, Professional Association of Innkeepers International, New Mexico Bed & Breakfast Association

RATED AAA 3 Diamonds, Mobil 3 Stars

KUDOS/COMMENTS "Comfortable and serene."

Dobson House

Hondo Mesa, Taos, NM 87571 *505-776-5738*
Joan & John Dobson, Innkeepers
EMAIL dobhouse@newmex.com
WEBSITE www.bbonline.com/nm/dobson

LOCATION From Taos, follow Highway 64 north toward Gorge Bridge. Turn right 0.3 mile past the Taos airport onto Tune Drive. Follow the signs to Dobson House.

OPEN All year

DESCRIPTION A 1995 solar adobe inn with Southwest decor, situated at 7,000 feet and overlooking the Rio Grande Gorge.

NO. OF ROOMS Three rooms with private bathrooms.

RATES Year-round rates are $100-115 for a single or double and $200 for a suite. There is a minimum stay during holidays and cancellation requires 14 days' notice with a $25 fee, 30 days' notice during holidays.

CREDIT CARDS No

BREAKFAST Full breakfast is served in the dining room and includes fresh fruit, juice, coffee, teas, Mexican baked eggs with chicken-apple sausage and spicy green onion–corn muffins, corn cakes and applewood-smoked bacon, or breakfast burritos. Dinner and picnic lunches are available, and vegan or vegetarian diets are accommodated.

AMENITIES Wine and hors d'oeuvres, coffee and tea tray in rooms before breakfast, hot springs a short hike away, extensive library, Rio Grande Gorge at end of drive, hiking and biking out the door, large common room available to guests, flowers.

RESTRICTIONS No smoking, no pets, children over 14 are welcome. The inn is not handicapped accessible. Pearl is the resident dog; Michael is the cat.

REVIEWED *The Santa Fe & Taos Book*

MEMBER Taos Association of Bed & Breakfast Inns, Professional Association of Innkeepers International

---

Don Pascual Martinez B&B

19 Valerio Road, Ranchos De Taos, NM 87557 *505-758-7364*

Dreamcatcher Bed & Breakfast

416 La Lomita, Taos, NM 87571 *505-758-0613*
Bob & Jill Purtee, Innkeepers *888-758-0613*
Some Spanish spoken *FAX 505-751-0115*
EMAIL dream@taosnm.com
WEBSITE www.taoswebb.com/hotel/dreamcatcher

LOCATION From historic Taos Plaza, take Don Fernando west for 0.3 mile. Turn right at the stop sign at San Antonio. The B&B is down the hill 0.1 mile.

OPEN All year

DESCRIPTION A 1947 adobe farm home with two additional casitas, decorated with southwestern decor and located on a wooded lot set back from the road.

NO. OF ROOMS Seven rooms with private bathrooms. Try the Pueblo.

RATES Year-round rates are $69-114 for a single or double and $129 for a suite. There is a minimum stay during holiday weekends and cancellation requires two weeks' notice.

CREDIT CARDS	American Express, Discover, MasterCard, Visa
BREAKFAST	Full breakfast is served in the dining room and includes cooked-to-order hot entrées such as green-chile breakfast burritos or cinnamon-raisin French toast. Fruit plates and cereals are offered each day.
AMENITIES	Hot tub under tall shade trees, hammocks and picnic table in the secluded courtyard, small refrigerators in rooms, plush robes, coffee-makers, ceiling fans. Each room has a wood-burning kiva or gas log fireplace.
RESTRICTIONS	No smoking, no pets, children over 10 are welcome. Allie is the resident dachshund. She is not allowed in guestrooms.
MEMBER	Professional Association of Innkeepers International, Taos Association of Bed & Breakfast Inns

Hacienda del Sol Bed & Breakfast

PO Box 177, Taos, NM 87571 — *505-758-0287*
Dennis Sheehan, Innkeeper — *FAX 505-758-5895*
EMAIL *sunhouse@newmex.com* — WEBSITE *www.taoshaciendadelsol.com*

LOCATION	One-and-a-half miles north of the Plaza on Paseo del Pueblo Norte. The private lane is next to the Southwest Moccasin and Drum Company.
OPEN	All year
DESCRIPTION	An 1810 pueblo revival–style inn surrounded by trees and gardens bordering on 9,500 acres of reservation land, with tremendous views of Taos Mountain.
NO. OF ROOMS	Eleven rooms with private bathrooms.
RATES	Year-round rates for a single, double, or suite are $75-155. There is a minimum stay on weekends and major holidays and cancellation requires 14 days' notice and a $15 fee.
CREDIT CARDS	MasterCard, Visa
BREAKFAST	Full breakfast, served in the dining room or on the patio, is prepared by the resident chef and features banana pancakes with maple syrup, special breakfast lasagna, breakfast tacos, homemade sticky buns, fresh juices, gourmet coffees, and more.
AMENITIES	Afternoon snacks, large outdoor Jacuzzi, robes, candy, cassette player with romantic tapes, champagne for special occasions, hot and cold beverages served at 5 p.m., three rooms have their own Jacuzzis, some rooms have private steam rooms, courtyards, spectacular views of Taos Mountain, facilities for weddings.

RESTRICTIONS	No smoking, no pets
REVIEWED	*Fodor's Southwest; Frommer's; Recommended Country Inns—The Southwest; Best Places to Stay in the Southwest; America's Wonderful Little Hotels & Inns*
MEMBER	Taos Bed & Breakfast Association, New Mexico Bed & Breakfast Association, Professional Association of Innkeepers International
RATED	AAA 3 Diamonds
AWARDS	One of the Ten Most Romantic Inns in the U.S., *USA Today*
KUDOS/COMMENTS	"Old hacienda with view of Taos Mountain, sprawling property." "True meaning of hospitality." (1996) "You can't find a more authentic New Mexico feeling." "Lovely large B&B bordering the pueblo."

INN ON LA LOMA PLAZA

315 Ranchitos Road, Taos, NM 87571 — *505-758-1717*
Jerry & Peggy Davis, Resident Owners — *FAX 505-758-4826*
WEBSITE www.taoswebb.com/laloma

KUDOS/COMMENTS	"Newly remodeled, private, walking distance to the Plaza." (1996)

INN ON THE RIO

910 Kit Carson Road, Taos, NM 87571 — *505-758-7199*
Julie & Robert Cahalane, Resident Owners — *800-859-6752*
Spanish spoken — *FAX 505-751-1816*
EMAIL innonrio@laplaza.org — *WEBSITE www.innontherio.com*

LOCATION	One-and-a-half miles east of the historic downtown Plaza, on Kit Carson Road (Highway 64 east).
OPEN	All year
DESCRIPTION	An adobe inn whose main building was constructed 250 years ago. The guestrooms were added in 1950. The interior is decorated in a comfortable Southwest style reflecting the rich and colorful local heritage. The inn is situated in a residential neighborhood beneath centuries-old silver cottonwoods.
NO. OF ROOMS	Twelve rooms with private bathrooms.
RATES	Year-round rates are $89-149 for a single or double. There is a minimum stay during Christmas and New Years. Please inquire about the cancellation policy.

Inn on the Rio, Taos

CREDIT CARDS	Discover, MasterCard, Visa
BREAKFAST	During the week, a creative, light, homemade breakfast is served in the cozy gathering room beside the Carmen Velardé kiva fireplace. A full hearty breakfast is served on weekends and holidays. Breakfasts are prepared by an authored gourmet cook.
AMENITIES	Snacks, fresh fruit, and beverages available throughout the day, outdoor hot tub with mountain views, heated pool, organic soap and lotion in private baths handpainted by a local folk artist, flower arrangements everywhere when the extensive gardens are in bloom.
RESTRICTIONS	No smoking, no pets. Little One, Shy Girl, Fuzzy Bear, and Mr. Brutus are the "official tail-waggers."
REVIEWED	*America's Favorite Inns, B&Bs, & Small Hotels; Fodor's; Rough Guide*
MEMBER	Taos Bed & Breakfast Inns
RATED	AAA 3 Diamonds

LA DONA LUZ INN

114 Kit Carson Road, Taos, NM 87571 *505-758-4874*
Nina Meyers & Paul Castillo, Resident Owners *800-758-9187*
Spanish spoken *FAX 505-758-4541*
EMAIL *info@ladonaluz.com* WEBSITE *www.ladonaluz.com*

LOCATION	Off the Plaza on Kit Carson Road.
OPEN	All year
DESCRIPTION	An 1802 three-story pueblo-style adobe inn decorated with old southwestern charm, with flower-filled patios, located in the heart of Taos with mountain views.
NO. OF ROOMS	Fifteen rooms with private bathrooms. The Rainbow Room is the best in the house.
RATES	Year-round rates for a single or double with a private bathroom are $59-189. There is a minimum stay over the Christmas holidays. Ask about a cancellation policy.
CREDIT CARDS	American Express, Discover, MasterCard, Visa
BREAKFAST	Continental plus is served in the dining room or on the patio and includes fresh blueberry muffins, cereals, strawberries with half-and-half or yogurt, orange juice, milk, coffee, and tea.
AMENITIES	Meeting facilities, four private hot tubs including one on the rooftop, cable TV with HBO, VCRs and videos, adobe fireplaces, air conditioning, two private kitchens, handicapped accessible, wishing well, patios.
RESTRICTIONS	None
REVIEWED	*Best Places to Stay in the Southwest; Destinations of the Southwest; Lonely Planet; The Complete Guide to Bed & Breakfasts, Inns, and Guesthouses in the United States, Canada, and Worldwide; Traveling with Pets; Best Places to Stay in the Southwest*
MEMBER	New Mexico Bed & Breakfast Association, New Mexico Hotel & Motel Association
RATED	Mobil 3 Stars

LA POSADA DE TAOS BED & BREAKFAST

309 Juanita Lane, Taos, NM 87571 — *505-758-8164*
Bill Swan, Innkeeper — *800-645-4803*
Spanish spoken — *FAX 505-751-3294*
EMAIL laposada@newmex.com — *WEBSITE www.taosnet.com/laposada*

LOCATION	Go west of the Plaza on Don Fernando for 2 blocks, turn left on Manzanares, drive 1 block and turn right on Juanita Lane. The B&B is at the end of the block, on the right.
OPEN	All year
DESCRIPTION	A 1907 two-story adobe with southwestern and country pine antiques and decorated with local art, situated in the historic district of Taos.
NO. OF ROOMS	Six rooms with private bathrooms. Try El Solecito Room.
RATES	March and May through October, rates are $95-135. Off-season rates are $75-120. There is no minimum stay. Ask about a cancellation policy.
CREDIT CARDS	American Express, Discover, MasterCard, Visa
BREAKFAST	Full breakfast is served in the dining room and includes juice, coffee, fruit, a hot entrée (such as pancakes, waffles, or egg dishes), and a side dish of meat.
AMENITIES	Fireplaces and private patios, advice on hiking and shopping.
RESTRICTIONS	No smoking, no pets, children over 12 are welcome.
REVIEWED	*Frommer's; Fodor's; Recommended Country Inns—The Southwest; Weekends for Two in the Southwest*
MEMBER	Taos Bed & Breakfast Association, Professional Association of Innkeepers International, New Mexico Bed & Breakfast Association
RATED	AAA 3 Diamonds, Mobil 3 Stars
KUDOS/COMMENTS	"Enjoyable, clean with wonderful hosts." "On a rare chance to get away from our B&B we stay here. The hosts are wonderful and the space and rooms delightful." (1996)

LAS PALOMAS DE TAOS

PO Box 3400, Taos, NM 87571 — *505-758-9456*

Laughing Horse Inn Bed & Breakfast

729 Del Pueblo Norte, Taos, NM 87571 *505-758-8350*

Little Tree Bed & Breakfast

226 Hondo-Seco Road, County Road B143, Taos, NM 87571 505 776-8467
Charles & Kay Giddens, Innkeepers
EMAIL little@newmex.com
WEBSITE www.littletreebandb.com

LOCATION	From the Taos Plaza, go north on Highway 64 for 4 miles, to the stoplight at the intersection with Highways 150 and 522. Take a right turn onto Highway 150, go 2.7 miles, turn left onto Highway 230 and go 1.9 miles. Turn left onto B143 (Hondo-Seco Road) and go exactly 2 miles. The B&B is on your left.
OPEN	All year
DESCRIPTION	A 1991 authentic hacienda-style adobe country inn with a walled courtyard and southwestern decor.
NO. OF ROOMS	Four rooms with private bathrooms. Try the Piñon Room.
RATES	Year-round rates are $80-105 for a single or double. There is a two-night minimum stay on weekends, three nights during major holidays, five nights at Christmas. Cancellation requires 10 days' notice.
CREDIT CARDS	American Express, Diners Club, Discover, MasterCard, Visa
BREAKFAST	Full breakfast is served in the dining room and includes juice, coffee, tea, fresh fruit, a hot entrée, homemade breads, muffins, pancakes, and more.
AMENITIES	Homemade cookies in rooms; complimentary snacks and sodas.
RESTRICTIONS	No smoking, no pets. Fred is the resident cat and official greeter.
REVIEWED	*Frommer's Santa Fe, Taos, & Albuquerque; Frommer's New Mexico; New Mexico's Best; Fodor's Bed & Breakfasts and Country Inns—The Southwest; Fodor's Gay Guide to the US*
MEMBER	Bed & Breakfast Inns of Taos
RATED	AAA 2 Diamonds
KUDOS/COMMENTS	"Built by owners, very attractive rooms, quiet location with beautiful views and sunny courtyard. Very good breakfasts and real sweet innkeepers." "On the outskirts of town, a semi-rural B&B which offers privacy in a delightful setting." (1996)

Mabel Dodge Luhan House

240 Morada Lane, Taos, NM 87571 — *505-751-9686*
EMAIL *mabel@taos.newmex.com* — WEBSITE *www.unink.com/mabel*

Mountain Light Bed & Breakfast

Altalaya Road, Arroyo Hondo, NM 87513 — *505-776-8474*
Gail Russell, Resident Owner
WEBSITE *www.mtnlight.com*

The Old Taos Guesthouse

1028 Witt Road, Taos, NM 87571 — *505-758-5448*
WEBSITE *www.taoswebb.com/hotel/oldtaoshouse/* — *800-758-5448*

LOCATION	From Taos Plaza, travel east on Kit Carson Road for 1.2 miles, then go right on Witt Road for 0.6 mile. The B&B is on the right side.
OPEN	All year
DESCRIPTION	An 1850 split-level, ranch-style adobe hacienda with southwestern furnishings located on 7.5 acres on a rise above Taos.
NO. OF ROOMS	Nine rooms with private bathrooms.
RATES	Year-round rates for a single or double are $70-125 and suites are $110-125. There is a two-night minimum stay during weekends and cancellation requires 10 days' notice.
CREDIT CARDS	MasterCard, Visa
BREAKFAST	Continental plus is served in the breakfast room and includes fresh-baked breads and muffins, hot or cold cereals with grains and fruit, juices, and coffee.
AMENITIES	Outdoor hot tub, rural atmosphere, quiet spots, fresh flowers, robes, expert local information, separate entrances.
RESTRICTIONS	No smoking, no pets.
REVIEWED	*Bed & Breakfast Guide—Southwest: Arizona, New Mexico, Texas; The Santa Fe & Taos Book; Fodor's Southwest; Recommended Country Inns of the Southwest; New Mexico* magazine; *Country* magazine

MEMBER Taos Bed & Breakfast Association

KUDOS/COMMENTS "Enchanting hot tub under the stars a treat. Hospitality and warmth of hosts superb." (1996)

Orinda

461 Valverde, Taos, NM 87571 *505-758-8581*
Adrian & Sheila Percival, Innkeepers *800-847-1837*
EMAIL *orinda@newmex.com* *FAX 505-751-4895*
WEBSITE *www.taosnet.com/orinda*

LOCATION Turn left off Highway 68 onto Civic Plaza Drive in town. At the stop sign (La Placita), turn right and take the first left (Valverde). Between the children's crossing and Valverde Park, our road drops downhill and to the right.

OPEN All year

DESCRIPTION A 1930s-era two-story adobe with southwestern furnishings and clerestory windows, situated on 2 acres with unobstructed views of Taos Mountain.

NO. OF ROOMS Five rooms with private bathrooms.

RATES Year-round rates are $80-145 for a single or double. Holiday rates are slightly more. There is no minimum stay and cancellation requires 14 days' notice.

CREDIT CARDS MasterCard, Visa

BREAKFAST Full breakfast is served in the dining room and includes a hot entrée, fresh fruit, and homemade breads.

AMENITIES Afternoon goodies, robes, soaps, sunblock, hammocks in summer, and fires in the winter

RESTRICTIONS No smoking, no pets, children over six are welcome.

REVIEWED *Fodor's Southwest; Frommer's Santa Fe, Taos, & Albuquerque; The Non-Smokers Guide to Bed & Breakfasts*

MEMBER Professional Association of Innkeepers International

KUDOS/COMMENTS "Small, intimate, rural setting with great views; great innkeepers." "Cozy three-bedroom with views of mesa and mountains." (1996)

Sagebrush Inn

1508 Paseo del Pueblo Sur, Taos, NM 87571 — *505-758-2254*
Ken & Louise Blair, Innkeepers — *800-428-3626*
Spanish, German, and French spoken — *FAX 505-758-5077*
EMAIL sagebrush@taos.newmex.com
WEBSITE www.taosweb.com/nmusa/taoshotels/sagebrushinn/

LOCATION	Three miles south of Taos Plaza, 1 mile north of historic Ranchos de Taos, and 0.5 mile north of the intersection of Highways 68 and 518.
OPEN	All year
DESCRIPTION	A 1929 three-story Mission-style pueblo adobe hotel decorated with handcarved Mexican furniture.
NO. OF ROOMS	One hundred rooms with private bathrooms.
RATES	January 29 through March 27, May 22 through October 19, and December 18 through January 2, rates are $85-95 for a single or double, and $125-140 for a suite. January 3 through January 28, March 28 through May 21, and October 20 through December 17, rates are $70-80 for a single or double, and $100-115 for a suite. There is a three-night minimum stay over Christmas. Cancellation requires two weeks' notice at Christmas.
CREDIT CARDS	American Express, Diners Club, Discover, MasterCard, Visa
BREAKFAST	Full breakfast is served in the dining room and includes eggs, pancakes, or French toast, with bacon, hashbrowns, toast, grapefruit, English muffin, orange juice, coffee, and tea.
AMENITIES	Live country-western music and dancing nightly, patio dining and barbecues for groups, two hot tubs, seasonal pool, 68 rooms with fireplaces, 26 rooms with balconies, designated pet rooms, handicapped accessible rooms, quiet courtyard rooms, conference facilities for up to 800, large art collection, health spa nearby, tennis club, and golf course.
RESTRICTIONS	None
REVIEWED	*Fodor's; Frommer's Santa Fe, Taos, & Albuquerque; Best Places to Stay in the Southwest; America's Wonderful Little Hotels & Inns*
RATED	AAA 2 Diamonds, Mobil 3 Stars

Salsa del Salto Bed & Breakfast Inn

543 Taos Ski Valley Road, Taos, NM 87529 — *505-776-2422*
Mary C. Hockett & Dadou Mayer, Resident Owners — *800-530-3097*
French, German, and Spanish spoken — *FAX 505-776-2422*
EMAIL salsa@newmex.com — *WEBSITE www.bandbtaos.com*

LOCATION	From the center of Taos, take Highway 64 north 4 miles to Highway 150 (Taos Ski Valley Road). Go right at 5.2 miles; the inn is on the right.
OPEN	All year
DESCRIPTION	A 1970–1992 southwestern contemporary inn with a two-story stone fireplace in the lobby and southwestern furnishings, with views of mountains and mesa.
NO. OF ROOMS	Ten rooms with private bathrooms.
RATES	Year-round rates for a single or double are $85-160. There is a minimum stay on weekends and holidays, and cancellation requires 14 days' notice.
CREDIT CARDS	MasterCard, Visa
BREAKFAST	Full breakfast, prepared by a French chef, is served in the dining room and includes a fruit, cereal, and yogurt buffet, followed by an entrée such as eggs Benedict, fresh-baked muffins, biscuits, and croissants.
AMENITIES	Lift tickets available at check-in, afternoon snacks, snow scraped from cars in the morning, snow reports, tennis court, swimming pool, hot tub, trail maps.
RESTRICTIONS	No smoking, no pets, children over six are welcome.
REVIEWED	*Fodor's; Frommer's; Inside Santa Fe and Taos; Best Places to Stay in the Southwest; Weekends for Two in the Southwest; Recommended Inns of the Southwest*
MEMBER	Taos Bed & Breakfast Association, New Mexico Bed & Breakfast Association, Professional Association of Innkeepers International
KUDOS/COMMENTS	"Nicely maintained property. Comfortable and good access to skiing." (1996)

San Geronimo Lodge

1101 Witt Road, Taos, NM 87571 — *505-751-3776*

Shady Brook

64 Shady Brook, Taos, NM 87571 — *505-751-1315*

Stewart House B&B

45 Highway 150, Taos, NM 87571 — *505-776-2557*
Carl & Sharon Fritz, Innkeepers — *888-505-2557*
Spanish and German spoken — *FAX 505-776-2557*
EMAIL stewarthouse@laplaza.org — *WEBSITE laplaza.org/~stwrths/*

LOCATION	Take Highway 68, 4.5 miles north of Taos, turn right at the light onto Highway 150, heading toward Taos Ski Valley. Drive 0.5 mile and look for the sign on the left.
OPEN	All year
DESCRIPTION	An eclectic, rambling wood-and-stone country inn with a warm and cozy, artistically eccentric interior, set on two acres with high desert all around and mountains on every side.
NO. OF ROOMS	Four rooms with private bathrooms.
RATES	Year-round rates are $65-115 for a single or double. There is a minimum stay during Christmas and New Years, and cancellation requires 10 days' notice.
CREDIT CARDS	American Express, Diners Club
BREAKFAST	Full breakfast is served and includes eggs or French toast with potatoes and bacon, plus breads, muffins, yogurt, fresh fruit salad, cereals, juice, milk, coffee, and teas.
AMENITIES	Hot tub, robes, meeting area available, handicapped accessible, fireplaces (one common, two in rooms).
RESTRICTIONS	No smoking, no pets
MEMBER	Taos Association of Bed & Breakfast Inns

Taos Country Inn at Rancho Rio Pueblo

Karavas and Ranchitos Road, Taos, NM 87571 — *505-758-4900*
WEBSITE www.taosnet.com/taoscountryinn — *800-866-6548*
FAX 505-758-4900

KUDOS/COMMENTS	"Yolanda Deveaux is as kind and pleasant as any person could ever be. The views from the inn are the best." (1996)

Taos Mountain Bed & Breakfast

15 El Salto Road, Arroyo Seco, NM 87514 — *505-776-8940*
Fab Torrez, Resident Owner — *FAX 505-776-1357*

Taos Mountain Outfitters Bed & Breakfast

131 Upper Ranchitos Road, Taos, NM 87571 — *505-758-8125*

Touchstone Inn & Destination Spa

11 Mabel Dodge Lane, Taos, NM 87571 — *505-758-0192*
Chloè Bren Price, Innkeeper — *800-758-0192*
Spanish spoken — *FAX 505-758-3498*
EMAIL touch@newmex.com — *WEBSITE www.taoswebb.com/touchstone*

LOCATION	Drive 1 mile north from the intersection of Highway 64/68 and Kit Carson. Go past the Laughing Horse Inn and turn right immediately after the Southwest Moccasin and Drum Shop. Go down the lane approximately 200 feet and turn into the drive to the right.
OPEN	All year
DESCRIPTION	A two-story traditional adobe inn with elegant, classic Southwest decor.
NO. OF ROOMS	Ten rooms with private bathrooms.
RATES	Year-round rates are $75-250 for a single or double. There is a two-night minimum stay on weekends, three nights during Christmas and New Years. Cancellation requires 14 days' notice, 30 days at Christmas and New Years.
CREDIT CARDS	American Express, MasterCard, Visa
BREAKFAST	Full gourmet vegetarian breakfast is served in the dining room or in the courtyard gallery with mountain views.
AMENITIES	Cable TV/VCR in every room, phones, outdoor hot tub, some rooms with Jacuzzi tubs, massage rooms, robes, coffee-makers, hair dryers.
RESTRICTIONS	No smoking, no pets, children over 12 are welcome. There is a resident outdoor chow.

REVIEWED	*Insiders' Guide to Santa Fe; Fodor's; America's Wonderful Little Hotels & Inns; Great Towns of America; Quick Escapes*
MEMBER	Professional Association of Innkeepers International, New Mexico Bed & Breakfast Association, Taos Association of Bed & Breakfast Inns
RATED	AAA 3 Diamonds, Mobil 3 Stars

The Willows Inn

412 Kit Carson Road at Dolan Street, Taos, NM 87571 — *505-758-2558*
Doug & Janet Camp, Resident Owners — *800-525-8267*
Spanish spoken — *FAX 505-758-5445*
EMAIL willows@newmex.com — *WEBSITE www.willows-taos.com*

LOCATION	From the Taos Plaza, travel east approximately 0.5 mile on Kit Carson Road (Highway 764) to the southeast corner of Kit Carson and Dolan Streets.
OPEN	All year
DESCRIPTION	A 1926 two-story pueblo-style adobe hacienda with Southwest and European decor, located on a 1-acre walled estate with gardens and two very large willow trees. Listed on the National and State Historic Registers.
NO. OF ROOMS	Five rooms with private bathrooms. The Camps recommend Henning's Studio.
RATES	Year-round rates for a single or double are $90-150. There is a minimum stay during holidays and cancellation requires 14 days' notice.
CREDIT CARDS	American Express, Discover, MasterCard, Visa
BREAKFAST	Full breakfast is served and includes three coffees, two juices, three cereals, tea, muffins or breakfast meat, fresh fruit, and an entrée such as blueberry pancakes, waffles, soufflés, or egg dishes.
AMENITIES	Decadent afternoon hospitality time complete with homemade baked goods, soups, and hors d'oeuvres; owner is an avid fly fisherman and guide who offers expert advice on local waters and instruction on fly tying and casting.
RESTRICTIONS	No smoking, no pets. The resident dachshunds are Sam and Annie, and the cat is Sebastian.
REVIEWED	*America's Wonderful Little Hotels & Inns; The Insiders' Guide to Santa Fe, Taos, and Albuquerque; Frommer's Santa Fe, Taos, & Albuquerque; Southwest—A Lonely Planet Travel Survival Kit; Recommended Country Inns—The Southwest*

MEMBER	Taos Bed & Breakfast Association, Professional Association of Innkeepers International
KUDOS/COMMENTS	"Real feeling of old Taos. Beautiful grounds and very nice innkeepers."

TAOS SKI VALLEY

AUSTING HAUS HOTEL

1282 State Highway 150, Taos Ski Valley, NM 87525 — *505-776-2649*
Paul Austing, Resident Owner — *800-748-2932*
Spanish and German spoken — *FAX 505-776-8751*

LOCATION	Five miles north of Taos, turn right onto State Highway 150. Go 13 miles on Highway 150; the hotel is on the left-hand side of the road.
OPEN	All year
DESCRIPTION	A 1985 two-story alpine country inn, surrounded by forest.
NO. OF ROOMS	Forty-five rooms with private bathrooms.
RATES	November through April, rates for a single or double are $108-165. May to mid-November, rates are $45-75 for a single or double. There is no minimum stay and cancellation in winter requires 30 days' notice, three days notice in the summer.
CREDIT CARDS	American Express, Discover, MasterCard, Visa
BREAKFAST	Continental plus is served in the dining room and includes a buffet of fruit, cereal, yogurt, pastries, cheeses, smoked salmon, bagels, coffee, tea, and juice. Dinner is also available during winter.
AMENITIES	Hair dryers, humidifier, cribs, barbecue grill, meeting room for groups of up to 50.
RESTRICTIONS	None. The resident basset hound is called Emy.
REVIEWED	*You Are Cordially Invited to the Best Choices in New Mexico; Best Places to Stay in the Southwest; Frommer's*

THOREAU

On the Continental Divide, a good jumping-off point for Chaco Canyon or Acoma (Sky City), and the oldest continuously inhabited city in the United States. Between Grants and Gallup on I-40.

ZUNI MOUNTAIN LODGE

HC-62, Thoreau, NM 87323 — *505-862-7769*
Richard E. Morrow & Robert A. McCuen, Resident Owners — *505-862-7616*
French and German spoken
EMAIL zuniml@cia-g.com
WEBSITE www.cia-g.com/~zuniml

LOCATION	Midway between Grants and Gallup on I-40. From Thoreau go 13 miles south on Highway 612, turn right at Peach Drive and go 0.4 mile west.
OPEN	All year
DESCRIPTION	A 1969 three-story territorial/Georgian with southwestern and some oriental interior furnishings, surrounded by piñon forest.
NO. OF ROOMS	Nine rooms with private bathrooms.
RATES	Year-round rates for a single or double are $55-85. There is no minimum stay and cancellation requires three days' notice.
CREDIT CARDS	No
BREAKFAST	Full breakfast is served in the dining room and includes waffles, muffins, omelets or scrambled eggs, fruit salad or melon, a selection of hot and cold cereals, juice, coffee, and tea. A full dinner is included in the room rate and a picnic lunch is available by reservation for $5.
AMENITIES	Private entrances, enclosed porches, full evening meal; tours to Chaco Canyon, El Morro, Canyon de Chelley, and elsewhere; juice bar, video collection, ground floor is handicapped accessible, mountain biking, horseshoes, basketball, volleyball, and croquet.
RESTRICTIONS	No smoking except on enclosed verandas and outdoors, no pets except with prior approval, children are welcome.
REVIEWED	*Hidden Southwest; Albuquerque Journal*

Tijeras

Lazy K Ranch Bed & Breakfast

Tijeras, NM 87059 *505-281-2072*

Truchas

A village halfway between Santa Fe and Taos on the High Road to Taos, Highway 76. The Milagro Beanfield War was filmed here.

Rancho Arriba Bed & Breakfast

373 County Road 75, Truchas, NM 87578 *505-689-2374*
Curtiss Frank, Resident Owner *FAX 505-689-2665*
Spanish spoken
EMAIL rancho@roadrunner.com
WEBSITE www.redbay.com/web/rancho

LOCATION	A half mile east of Truchas on County Road 75.
OPEN	All year
DESCRIPTION	A 1965 traditional adobe hacienda built around a plaza, located on a farm 8 miles from 13,000-foot mountain peaks and overlooking the Rio Grande valley. The interior features white plaster walls, corner fireplaces, and homemade southwestern furniture.
NO. OF ROOMS	Three rooms share two-and-a-half bathrooms.
RATES	Year-round rates are $50 for a single and $70 for a double. There is no minimum stay and cancellation requires one week's notice.
CREDIT CARDS	MasterCard, Visa
BREAKFAST	Full breakfast is served in the dining room and includes farm-fresh eggs, bacon, toast, fresh-ground coffee, and tea.
AMENITIES	Robes, porch with a view, hay fields to walk in.
RESTRICTIONS	Smoking outside only, no pets. Ballet and Chico are the resident quarter horses, and there are numerous cats on the property.
MEMBER	New Mexico Bed & Breakfast Association

Rancho del Llano Bed & Breakfast

PO Box 405, Truchas, NM 87578 *505-689-2347*
EMAIL *vmarkley@la-tierra.com* WEBSITE *www.la-tierra.com/vmarkley/*

Tularosa

Pecan Tree

802 Old Mescalero Road, Tularosa, NM 88352 *505-585-2238*

White Rock

Back Porch Bed & Breakfast

13 Karen Circle, White Rock, NM 87544 *505-672-9816*
Shirley Webb, Resident Owner

INDEX

G–H

I–K

L

M

N–P

R

S

T

U–Z